What people are saying about *The Nonprofit Guide to S*

If you are serious, and I mean serious, about learning how to implement a successful earned income venture, this is the book you need: a step-by-step workbook that includes a proven methodology I've used for the past eight years in my consulting practice. Using the tools described, I've helped dozens of nonprofits integrate earned income strategies into their organizational culture and launch successful social enterprise ventures.

Cindy Kane
President, GW Group Inc.

Social: occupied with matters of human welfare. Enterprise: systematic and industrious activity; an undertaking, especially one of great scope. Most nonprofit organizations encounter these words on a daily basis but not together. Now there is a way to strategically align the funding for your mission. It is called social enterprise.

Jim Copeland
Executive Director, Alta Mira Specialized Family Services

This upbeat, detailed, user-friendly manual is a clarion call to nonprofits: wake up to the new world of raising funds through social entrepreneurship before it's too late. Jean Block and Niki McCuistion present case studies and sample business plans to demystify the process and open up a window of opportunity for any organization.

Irene Webb
President, IW Development

Are you tired of funders driving your bus? Jean Block and Niki McCuistion's exciting new book will put you back in the driver's seat to transition from "business as usual" to financial freedom and sustainability. The Nonprofit Guide to Social Enterprise is an investment that you won't want to pass up. It will guide you through the process of becoming more independent, less vulnerable, more creative, and more sustainable, giving you solid steps to a new model that diversifies your funding portfolio and increases your competitive advantage.

Janette Monear
President and CEO, Texas Trees Foundation

Without a doubt, all nonprofits will sooner than later need to look at sound and proven methods of financially expanding their nonprofits. Jean Block and Niki McCuistion's book views all aspects of social enterprise and sustainability that are so essential in an environment that offers fewer funding opportunities for nonprofits no matter how important their noble cause is. This book is timely and offers practical how-tos to help nonprofits understand the importance of looking at their organizations with the business "hats" they need to succeed in today's funding environment and implement the strategies that will keep them viable and vibrant. The authors know the funding marketplace and give solid advice on how to succeed in today's competitive and challenging environment.

Beverly Weurding, MBA
Founder and CEO, Wheelchair Dancers Organization

Get ready to roll up your sleeves and be successful with social enterprise. Plenty of books have been written on the theory, value, and need for SE, but few have provided a road map to take you from business as usual to profitability. Through this honest and thorough assessment, you'll gain a clear understanding of if and why social enterprise is a good fit for your organization.

Ruth Ann Greuling, MA
College Instructor and Social Enterprise Catalyst

This is must reading for any nonprofit leaders (paid or volunteer) who want to ensure their organizations are relevant and sustainable. The simple yet serious self-assessment tools in this book should be followed for existing programs as well as those (perhaps before) branching into new enterprises. The authors have provided a clear guidebook to help nonprofits cut through the chatter around social enterprise and actually enjoy the benefits to their agencies and clients of engaging in the process of becoming social entrepreneurs. I recommend this as background reading for your next strategic planning initiative. Not sold? Read the first and tenth chapters, and you will be.

Cathy Packard
Social Entrepreneur and Nonprofit Executive

The Nonprofit Guide to Social Enterprise *masterfully combines cutting-edge information to show how nonprofit fundraisers can achieve long-term sustainable revenue streams for their organizations. As part of a comprehensive fundraising system, the science of social enterprise as described by* The Nonprofit Guide to Social Enterprise *is an essential complement to the art of nonprofit fundraising. I can't wait to get started on the workbook!*

Patricia Melton
Director of Development and Communications, Metro Dallas Homeless Alliance

Whether you are launching a start-up as a new social entrepreneur or contemplating ways to reinvigorate an existing enterprise, this practical workbook will take you through the essential considerations of a well-conceived, executable plan.

Steve Carlson
COO Cafe Momentum (a virtual social enterprise)

Jean Block and Niki McCuistion's must-read/must-follow manual is perfect for any organization looking to implement a social enterprise. This practical guide prompts the reader to take a critical look at their social enterprise idea from conception to implementation and gives the reader all the tools and worksheets needed to stay on track.

Katie Hanners
Senior Director of Social Enterprise, Catholic Charities Fort Worth

If your organization is serious about its long-term existence and finding alternative streams of income, I heartily recommend the social enterprise process. As a fellow traveler interested in making a difference in this world, I invite you to take the expedition.

Margaret Ann Hoogstra
Executive Director, Texas Forts Trail

The Nonprofit Guide to Social Enterprise

Show Me the (Unrestricted) Money!

Jean Block
Niki Nicastro McCuistion

The Nonprofit Guide to Social Enterprise: Show Me the (Unrestricted) Money!

One of the **In the Trenches**™ series

Published by
CharityChannel Press, an imprint of CharityChannel LLC
30021 Tomas, Suite 300
Rancho Santa Margarita, CA 92688-2128 USA

charitychannel.com

In the Trenches, In the Trenches logo, and book design are trademarks of CharityChannel Press, an imprint of CharityChannel LLC.

ISBN Print Book: 978-1-938077-44-9 | ISBN eBook: 978-1-938077-45-6

Library of Congress Control Number: 2013957579

13 12 11 10 9 8 7 6 5 4 3 2 1

Printed in the United States of America

This and most CharityChannel Press books are available at special quantity discounts for bulk purchases for sales promotions, premiums, fundraising, or educational use. For information, contact CharityChannel Press, 30021 Tomas, Suite 300, Rancho Santa Margarita, CA 92688-2128 USA. +1 949-589-5938

Publisher's Acknowledgments

This book was produced by a team dedicated to excellence; please send your feedback to editors@charitychannel.com.

We first wish to acknowledge the tens of thousands of peers who call charitychannel.com their online professional home. Your enthusiastic support for the **In the Trenches**™ series is the wind in our sails.

Members of the team who produced this book include:

Editors

Acquisitions Editor: Linda Lysakowski

Comprehensive Editor: Stephen Nill

Copy Editor: Jill McLain

Production

In the Trenches Series Design: Deborah Perdue

Layout Editor: Jill McLain

Administrative

CharityChannel LLC: Stephen Nill, CEO

Marketing and Public Relations: John Millen

About the Authors

Jean Block

Jean is a nationally known consultant, trainer, and author on nonprofit management, FUNdraising, board development, and social enterprise. She has been an executive director and board chair for local, regional, and national nonprofits. She learned about social enterprise in 2003 and taught a six- to nine-month program on social enterprise through a contract with the National Center for Social Entrepreneurs. In 2006, she formed Social Enterprise Ventures, LLC, as a part of her long-standing consulting company, Jean Block Consulting, Inc. Jean has taught social enterprise to more than one hundred nonprofits throughout the United States, many of which have already launched very successful earned income ventures. She speaks to hundreds of nonprofit professionals each year.

Jean is the author of *Expedition*, a hands-on manual on social enterprise, *The Invisible Yellow Line: Clarifying Board and Staff Roles*, *The ABCs of Building Better Boards*, *Fast FUNdraising Facts for Fame and Fortune*, and *FUNdraising! 180+ Great Ideas to Raise More Money*, as well as numerous articles and other nonprofit resources.

Niki Nicastro McCuistion

Niki is a consultant, speaker, executive coach, and author who focuses on performance strategies that help organizations and individuals achieve sustainable results. Over the last twenty-five years, she has provided strategic business consulting and coaching, nationally and internationally, to thousands of corporate executives, entrepreneurs, and their management teams, with a focus on nonprofit governance and strategy, change management, leadership, and fundraising. As a former nonprofit CEO, she was responsible for all facets of its fundraising and understands firsthand the many challenges nonprofits experience. Niki has earned the highest professional award the National Speakers' Association bestows, the CSP (Certified Speaking Professional).

She is the author/coauthor of several business books on sales, leadership, coaching, and change management, as well as numerous business articles. Her latest book, *Women, Wealth and Giving*, is a model for philanthropic business development strategies.

Niki earned a master of philanthropy and development from St. Mary's University, Winona, Minnesota, and an MBA from the University of Dallas in nonprofit leadership and governance. She is working on her certified fundraising executive designation.

Dedication

We dedicate this manual to America's hard-working nonprofit organizations that strive daily to make our country and the world a better place to live, work, and raise our families. We hold these dedicated nonprofits in the highest esteem as they continue their efforts to make this world a better place for us all. Your services are needed now more than ever.

Your missions are critical, and we salute you.

Authors' Acknowledgments

We've been CEOs of nonprofits, and we've been entrepreneurs; we've helped run large and small nonprofit organizations; and we've struggled to build capacity and sustain ourselves in good times and in lean times. We serve on nonprofit boards, and we have felt and acted on the strong desire to improve the circumstances of those nonprofits we've served.

We've learned from mentors in traditional and nontraditional nonprofit management. Some of our finest mentors have led us to the understanding that as the world around us changes, so too must our nonprofits change if they are to survive and sustain themselves and their missions.

We believe a new culture in the nonprofit sector that rewards innovation, sustainability, and profitability must be created. There simply is no choice if nonprofits are to continue being impactful. It's obvious, to any who pay attention, that the current model of philanthropy is broken. There are too many demands for services and too few resources to meet them. Nonprofits must shift from a starvation cycle to one that makes a profit leading from the heart so they are capable of fulfilling their missions with the revenues to do so.

This manual is the result of many experiences. It's built on the foundation of the Social Enterprise Ventures LLC team, the nonprofits we've managed, and the many clients we've worked with who deeply believe in and work for their organization's purpose. It takes a community to write a book, and we are grateful to everyone who participated and helped us understand that it's time to dramatically change the way nonprofits operate.

Thank you, each and every one, for your generosity of spirit and giving.

Contents

Summary of Chapters

Chapter One
Social Enterprise: Changing the World for the Common Good. This chapter will give a brief history of philanthropy, discuss the landscape in the nonprofit fundraising community today, provide an overview of social enterprise, define the various kinds of social enterprises, and make a case for nonprofit organizations to explore how social enterprise could be of value to their missions.

Chapter Two
Paradigm Shifts: The Business of Doing Good. We'll examine the perils, pitfalls, paradoxes, and successes involved in social enterprise and compare nonprofit with for-profit key functions so that you can evaluate the pluses and minuses of social enterprise for yourself, given the present composition of your organization. We will further define business planning and why we believe it's an essential success ingredient in today's nonprofit climate.

Chapter Three
Vetting the Social Enterprise Model. This chapter will outline the questions that must be addressed prior to your organization embarking on a social enterprise business model that will be a workable one for your needs. It will examine funding and sustainability models, tax exemption, governance, and the various structures that impact a journey to social enterprise.

Chapter Four
Organizational Goals, Focus, and Desired Outcomes. Using hands-on exercises, this chapter will explore the basics of social enterprise as it relates to your organization and help you decide on the need, if any, for change. It will challenge the various assumptions you may have about your organization and help clarify what has brought you to the point of social enterprise exploration.

Chapter Five
Examining Your Assets and Opportunities: What You Do, What You Have, What You Know.
This chapter will help you identify your organization's core competencies, develop objective

criteria, and brainstorm potential opportunities for social enterprise. It will prompt what has to be done differently to achieve desired outcomes and discover implementation processes that lead to results.

Chapter Six

Testing the Water. This chapter will provide hands-on tools to perform the market research to test the assumptions made so far and confirm you can identify a viable earned income opportunity. It will define a market research process to explore your potential customer base and will outline a systematic market analysis that must be conducted to determine the kinds of products, services, or programs that will be offered. You'll also explore the benefits, price, promoting, and advertising of chosen products and how to evaluate your competition.

Chapter Seven

Developing Your Sales Plan. You can have the greatest social enterprise in the world, but if potential customers don't know about it or can't find it, your hard work is wasted and your profitability is a dream. This chapter will clarify everything you learned in market research and help you develop a successful sales plan to reach your target market.

Chapter Eight

Understanding Pricing, Financing, and Costs. An often-overlooked component in evaluating the viability and sustainability of an earned income venture is calculating the real and total costs necessary to operate and maintain these separate operations, programs, and services. Knowing true costs is imperative for pricing products and services accurately. Price them too low, and you lose money; too high, and you price yourself out of the market. This chapter will help you accurately identify all categories of costs, allocating those costs appropriately to determine the break-even and profit points for your social enterprise.

Chapter Nine

Developing Your Business Plan. Successful ventures have business plans that encompass the who, what, why, where, and when of the venture. This chapter will provide guidance on how a business plan is developed and walk you through the basic pieces required for a full business plan. Worksheets will provide a clear snapshot of how a plan needs to be structured to allow for success and evaluation. The plan will serve as a basis to track and ensure the success of the earned income venture.

Chapter Ten

Sustainability: The End Goal. This workbook provides models and hands-on guides for those who want to explore earned income revenue streams to help generate the revenue that allows you to fulfill your mission outside of and in addition to traditional funding models. In this chapter, we will refer to case studies and stories of others' successes and challenges. We will finalize our case in support for social enterprise, why we believe it is a viable alternative, and include the backup data to support this premise.

Foreword

Lao-tzu once said, "Every journey of a thousand miles begins with the first step." Well, thanks to the insights outlined in Jean Block's and Niki Nicastro McCuistion's *The Nonprofit Guide to Social Enterprise*, the intimidating journey of launching a social enterprise is a walk in the park. Or at least it feels like one. Thank goodness.

In an economic time when government support and philanthropic dollars from the corporate sector are growing tighter, it has become more important than ever for nonprofits to develop alternative revenue streams if they are to be sustainable. Jean and Niki have put together an extensive cookbook of recipes to help nonprofits determine whether social enterprise should be part of their diet and, if so, which combination of ingredients will work best for them. Nonprofits, like any business, need to be mindful of where every dollar is spent, and by using the tools provided in this book, an organization can save thousands of dollars while building a business model that will generate unrestricted revenue for years to come.

I only wish that Jean and Niki had written this book when I was first launching my career in the nonprofit sector. More than twenty years ago, I had the good fortune to land a job with an innovative nonprofit national service organization, City Year, that was developed by two Harvard Law School graduates. The "good news" is that City Year's cofounders, Michael Brown and Alan Khazei, recognized early on that the organization would not be able to, nor did it choose to, rely on the government to provide sole funding for the program. It would be imperative for corporations, foundations, and individuals to buy into the concept as well if we wanted it to be around for generations of young people to dedicate a year or two to community service.

Although it didn't have a name back then, Alan, Michael, and a team of experts at the Timberland Company spent many hours, creative bandwidth, and lots of dollars developing what we would clearly now refer to as a social enterprise. If only we had *The Nonprofit Guide to Social Enterprise* as our playbook, we could have invested all of those resources in strengthening our communities and addressing critical social needs.

As someone who has been in the nonprofit industry doing fundraising for more than two decades, I want to give Jean and Niki a heartfelt "thank-you" for finally putting together such a wonderful manual on social enterprise. Through their clever writing style, they provide the how-tos in a way that makes a potentially very intimidating and even paralyzing process feel completely doable. They recognize that identifying and developing a social enterprise requires understanding, customization, and—most of all—simple steps. And that's what they stay focused on, making it simple to do good.

Jean and Niki, thank you for generating this inspiring conversation about leveraging the entrepreneurial spirit of the nonprofit community. Once enough readers get this book in their hands, we will all undoubtedly feel the deprivation model of the nonprofit community smoothly shift to one of unstoppable recurring revenue.

Pam Gerber, Executive Director
Entrepreneurs For North Texas

Introduction

Nonprofits are in a big transition. This transition paves the way for social enterprise as more sustainable modes of revenue and sustainability are explored. Social enterprise is one of those avenues that can assist a nonprofit in governing its own future.

A social enterprise is a business whose primary purpose is the common good. According to the Social Enterprise Alliance, a social enterprise uses the methods and disciplines of business and the power of the marketplace to advance its social, environmental, and human justice agendas. It is important to clearly understand that social enterprise addresses an intractable social need and that commercial activity is a strong revenue driver. The goal of social enterprise is to build a more sustainable world by applying market-based strategies and workable business models to today's social problems. We'll discuss this in more detail further on.

So, are you ready for social enterprise? You are if your board and staff leadership has embraced the change from *charity-think* to *tax-exempt business-think*. You are if your board and staff leadership will commit the time and dollar resources necessary to invest in the process of social enterprise.

That's right—it takes time, money, and an innovative mindset to launch a successful social enterprise business venture. This manual is a guide through the process of change required to become a successful social entrepreneur. It is based on a copyrighted training manual that we've used successfully for more than ten years.

This manual outlines the seven key steps required to launch an earned income venture. Each chapter contains detailed worksheets to guide you through the process. Use the worksheets provided as is or as a guide to create your own. But don't be tempted to short-cut the critical steps! To do so would put your valuable organizational assets at risk.

This process takes time to do right. You can expect to spend at least six to nine months from start to finish. The critical market research and feasibility study phases will take most of that time and are necessary for good results.

Many nonprofit organizations have followed the process outlined in this manual and have reaped the benefits of generating unrestricted renewable income. They have weathered the downturns in traditional funding without reducing staff or compromising programs.

Nonprofit organizations that have the discipline, flexibility, innovation, creativity, and new way of thinking required to undertake this process from start to finish—and that hold themselves responsible for following this manual from beginning to end—will celebrate the successful launch of a social enterprise.

Many, however, will find it difficult to find the discipline required and will need a mentor, guide, experienced consultant, or training team to help them stay on track. Don't be afraid to ask for help!

Chapter One

Social Enterprise: Changing the World for the Common Good

IN THIS CHAPTER

····→ Philanthropy is changing

····→ What is social enterprise?

····→ Why a social enterprise model?

····→ Trends in social enterprise

Philanthropy: A Core American Value

Americans are some of the most generous people in the world. Charitable giving is a central part of the American fabric. Americans consistently give away approximately 2 percent of their disposable income, regardless of whether it's during good or tough times. In fact, more Americans donate to charity than vote.

Philanthropy is a core American value, crossing over socioeconomic, gender, and racial divides. Charity goes back to our founding settlers, who gave even when they had little for themselves. John Winthrop, one of the leading figures in the founding of the Massachusetts Bay Colony (1629), set the foundation of philanthropy as a core value when he counseled settlers that "We must bear one another's burden . . . and the care of the public must take precedence over all private interests."

Today, these values are still our bedrock. During this last recession, Razoo (razoo.com), a crowd funding source for nonprofits that continually surveys its clients, surveyed 2,059 adults on their

> *The raising of extraordinarily large sums of money given voluntarily and freely by millions of Americans is a unique American tradition... Philanthropy... charity, giving, call it what you like, but it is truly a jewel of American tradition.*
>
> John F. Kennedy

holiday charitable giving. The survey pointed out that of those who were unemployed, 47 percent said they would still be donating to charity.

Robert L. Payton, former director of the Center of Philanthropy at Indiana University, said, "It is no surprise that philanthropy is the principal means by which our ethics and values shape the society in which we live." Philanthropy is at the heart of who we are as a society and it is undeterred by hardship and challenging economic times.

Giving USA (givingusareports.org) has stated, "Individual Americans and our country's foundations and corporations continue to be generous during a time of slow economic growth."

However, since the 2008 recession, research has shown many nonprofit organizations just how vulnerable they are. Depending on charitable contributions, often from the same resources, or hoping the next government grant would come in resulted in more than one nonprofit closing its doors or cutting its operational expenses to the bone.

Too Many Issues and Too Few Dollars

If you've picked up this manual, in all likelihood you agree that philanthropy is a core American value and that Americans are generous. But the challenges of the last recession and the fallout you may still be dealing with have perhaps caused you to say, "Enough! There has to be a way to sustain our organization rather than being dependent solely on charity." Without nonprofits, there would be even more of a challenge in solving social issues. Yes, philanthropy is a core value, but it's even more than this. The work of nonprofits wouldn't get done otherwise, and there would be an even greater gap for services, which would affect our overall quality of life.

The volatility of our economy has impacted giving as we now know it, and it will continue to have an impact. The last several years have challenged philanthropic giving and taken their toll. The handwriting has been on the wall for quite a while, yet many nonprofits have virtually ignored the signs. Giving USA has repeatedly told us that total charitable giving may have increased in current dollars and picked up again, but the giving picture has been flat for some time.

Yet Patrick Rooney, PhD, executive director for the Center on Philanthropy at Indiana University, warned us, "This is going to be a tough era... It will be ten years before we [nonprofits] regain the ground we have lost, or five times the recovery time experienced earlier in this decade" (*Nonprofit Quarterly*, January 2013). Did we pay attention, or did we go about business as usual, ignoring obvious signs?

In our last recession, Daring to Lead, a national study of nonprofit executive leadership, reported that 84 percent of nonprofits were negatively impacted, with 46 percent reporting cash reserves on hand of less than three months.

There is no doubt that government is less willing to pay for social services and allow tax credits and that many nonprofits are in jeopardy. Sequestration and charitable-deduction issues continue to chip away at giving. As a result, your role becomes even more important.

The nonprofit sector is a critical and necessary part of our economy, speaking for those who cannot speak for themselves. Society's needs are greater than ever. US nonprofit sector revenue alone represents the eleventh-largest economy in the world, ahead of Australia, Mexico, and Russia. US nonprofits also account for 9.2 percent of all wages and salaries paid in the United States, currently contributing more than $1.51 trillion in total revenues to our economy.

Today, many nonprofit organizations are at a crossroads. They are cutting their operating expenses to the bone, existing day to day, risking the quality of work that gets done, and putting greater stress on staff. Balancing your organization's financial goals and its social mission is increasingly difficult. The need society has for your services is huge and demand for services is up, yet many nonprofits are operating with a diminishing pot of dollars to serve and solve social problems. Nonprofits that operate in "business as usual" mode can't succeed if too many more cuts are made.

It doesn't have to be this way. And if this manual is in your hands, then you may be looking for a better way that takes you beyond subsistence to sustainability. For a nonprofit such as yours to succeed in fulfilling your mission, the old ways—relying on charitable contributions, special events, government grants, and subsidies—are no longer the only answers.

We propose that for a growing number of nonprofits, finding alternatives to traditional ways of keeping the doors open is imperative. We believe it is critical that nonprofits develop a sustainable business model to attain the funding

> It bears repeating that the old funding model, which for some was nothing short of begging, is no longer a viable option. But then, it never was.
>
>
> important

needed to fulfill their mission and allow for growth. The old model, which for some was nothing short of begging, is no longer a viable option. We argue that it was never a viable option, as it restricted the ability to compete effectively. Diversifying the funding portfolio and reducing cash-flow stress is essential to future success.

Social Enterprise as a Viable Option

We know from experience that the process we are offering in this manual can bring you success. We've seen the successful outcomes that can result. Our philosophy, and we stand firmly behind it, is that by adopting the business practices we teach in this manual, you can be sustainable. There is no doubt that by consistently putting into practice the processes we talk about, you will strengthen your organization and better achieve your desired outcomes.

As resources continue to dry up and expectations increase for an ROI, nonprofits that more strategically embrace alternative sources of funding will increase their sustainability and revolutionize the nonprofit world. This move toward a different way of funding is encouraging nonprofits to explore the concepts of social enterprise as a possible solution.

We've emphasized that the goal of social enterprise is to build a more sustainable world by applying market-based strategies and workable business models to today's social problems. At the forefront of this movement is the Social Enterprise Alliance (SEA). As we have mentioned, SEA defines a social enterprise as "an organization or venture that advances its primary social or environmental mission using business methods." SEA states that there are three characteristics that distinguish a social enterprise:

◆ It directly addresses an intractable social need and serves the common good, either through its products and services or through the number of "disadvantaged" people it employs.

◆ Its commercial activity is a strong revenue driver, whether a significant earned revenue stream within a nonprofit's mixed-revenue portfolio or a for-profit enterprise.

> Social enterprise is not about turning your nonprofit into a for-profit corporation. Rather, it is about applying sound business principles to how you manage your nonprofit business, because that is what you are—a business.
>
> **observation**

◆ The common good is the primary purpose, literally "baked into" the organization's DNA and trumping all others.

A caveat: Social enterprise is not about turning nonprofits into hard-core entrepreneurial businesses. It's also not about "business as usual." We have learned that by applying business models and strategies, nonprofits such as yours can build a sustainable model that will not leave you so heavily reliant on funding that may no longer exist or over which you have little or no control. Our goal with this manual is to introduce you to these models, show concrete examples, and give you case studies and strategies, plans, worksheets, and assessments so you may decide for yourself if social enterprise is a viable alternative for your organization and one of the solutions you apply to attaining your organization's mission. We are also the first to caution that while social enterprise is a viable solution, it is not the only solution, and it's certainly not for everyone.

The Case for Social Enterprise

It seems the list of overwhelming social, environmental, and human concerns is growing far more quickly than the ability of traditional nonprofits to address them. SEA says that "the social enterprise sector is emerging as the 'missing middle,' stepping into the void between the traditional worlds of government, nonprofits, and business." They remind us that government doesn't have the resources, nor is it government's role to solve every social problem. Nonprofits are faced with declining revenue sources and demands for measurement and impact they weren't facing before, and business's job is to increase shareholder profits.

At its best, social enterprises can address these concerns more efficiently than traditional government programs and more sustainably than traditionally funded nonprofits, using business best practices while serving the common good. Social enterprises are a powerful engine for economic and social development that directly address social needs through products, services, or the numbers of people they employ. And their purpose is still to make the world a better place. A social enterprise's success should be evaluated on its ability to fulfill its promises, not on its ability to beg for funding and "prove" how little money it needs to run the operation. A starvation diet isn't necessary.

Social enterprise is not an easy task. It is important work that must have the full backing of your leadership, at both the staff level and the board level, if your organization is to:

◆ attain sustainability;

◆ realize it's no longer viable to operate in business-as-usual mode;

◆ implement a different revenue-generating model;

◆ recognize that 501(c)(3) is a tax designation, not a business plan;

◆ create new income streams; or

◆ expand your services.

> "Nonprofit" is merely a tax designation. It is not a sound business plan or model.
>
>

The economic environment has forced nonprofits to seriously evaluate how they fulfill their missions. We know that the overall funding climate has changed. Competition for donations is up, with more nonprofits vying for a piece of the funding pie, and government has cut back on social spending only to depend on the public sector to fill the gap. Yet is this realistic? Where will the money come from? The writing has been on the wall for a while, and as we said earlier, we've ignored it to a large degree.

Nonprofits have traditionally underreported their real cost of doing business, being forced to fulfill their mission with little money for actual overhead and competitive pay, creating a "we'll just make do" culture. Reality has finally caught up. In a *Social Innovation Review* article in the fall of 2009, Ann Coggins Gregory and Don Howard state, "A vicious cycle is leaving nonprofits so hungry for decent infrastructure that they can barely function as organizations, let alone serve their beneficiaries." This has come to be known as the starvation cycle, and if anything is true, it has gotten worse, not better.

Please keep in mind that while our primary focus is on nonprofits earning revenue to fulfill their mission, social enterprise is not the exclusive domain of nonprofits. There are several different types of social enterprises, nonprofit and for-profit. The models work for both.

Types of Social Enterprises

1. Social purpose businesses can be nonprofit, for-profit, a public/private partnership, or some combination of these three.

2. Earned income businesses have a direct impact on a social need. These are revenue-generating activities started by nonprofits that may be related or unrelated to their core business, such as the organization renting out its facility during downtime, gift shops that are part of the enterprise, accounting expertise and consulting, catering, cafeterias, and so on.

   Note: While your social enterprise can exist as part of your nonprofit, some organizations will move their social enterprise at some point to a for-profit corporation. This can be a viable option if the social enterprise generates significant revenue or requires significant agency resources.

3. Business partnerships between nonprofits and for-profits, as in cause-related marketing and cause-related purchasing programs.

4. Other earned income strategies. Business ventures and partnerships such as community development entrepreneurial efforts by government agencies.

Keep in mind this fundamental premise: While a social enterprise may achieve its primary mission using sound business methods, it is not primarily motivated by profit. Its goal is centered on "doing good": curing maladies, addressing social needs, helping those who are outside of the socioeconomic mainstream, etc.

Missions Need Money

For too long, nonprofits have operated with a mindset that claimed they could not take advantage of business models that would allow them the financial resources to fund their missions. "Making do," not making a profit, has been encouraged, and we laud the nonprofits that spend next to nothing on their infrastructure as the models that could be followed. On the other hand, we applaud successful businesses that are profitable, but at the same time, we look down on them as greedy capitalists who exploit society.

Yes, we may be speaking the unspeakable, what some would call nonprofit heresy, and yet avoiding the elephant in the room spells peril for thousands of nonprofits. The good old days are gone. It's time to realize that one of the best ways your nonprofit can realize your mission is to thoroughly investigate the benefits of social enterprise.

Here is what we know and you will be reminded of often in this manual: Being a nonprofit 501(c)(3) is merely a tax designation. To succeed in implementing your organization's mission, you must have the appropriate capital.

Too many small- to average-sized nonprofits operate with less than thirty to ninety days of reserves. It's difficult, if not impossible, to solve problems, be creative, or expand your programs when you're having to nickel and dime everything and can't afford enough staff to get the job done.

Trends in Social Enterprise

If our case for social enterprise doesn't convince you of its viability and value, consider these important trends:

◆ The social innovation movement is growing and will open up more opportunities for social enterprises. Deloitte, one of the world's leading business consulting companies, recently added a corporate innovations manager, giving witness to its power and influence.

◆ Now might be the optimum time for your nonprofit to consider social enterprise because numerous economic factors are in play that will support this step toward your sustainability.

◆ Reduced funding from grants and government is forcing nonprofits to seek other types of funding, particularly ones over which they have more control. This increases competition as well, as there are new nonprofits forming daily. Social enterprise is one such source.

◆ The number of highly skilled businesspeople who are unemployed has risen sharply since the recession began in 2007. This labor pool means that nonprofits stand a better chance of attracting people with the needed skills to start and run their social enterprises.

◆ In 2010, President Obama created the White House Office of Social Innovation, which is dedicated to supporting and convening all sectors of society (nonprofits, government, NGOs, private sector, and individuals) to work together to find solutions to the many problems facing our country. More partnering and collaborations are encouraged.

◆ As funding to nonprofits has diminished, the funding community has stepped up its requirements for outcome measurements. Nonprofits are expected to show more tangible impact.

◆ The added "return on investment" (ROI) scrutiny of the nonprofit sector may prevent some nonprofits from qualifying as typical foundation grantees, and many individual funders rarely provide the needed financial support for necessary business activities, including technology, infrastructure, marketing, strategy, and staffing. In other words, they don't want to fund operational expenses. Too often their donations are for mission-only outcomes.

For a moment, pause. Please. This last statement leaves us breathless, and not in a good way. Can you imagine Apple's investors not funding operating expenses? Can you imagine Apple not hiring the brightest and best thinkers, innovators, creators, engineers, software people—everything it takes to get an iPad to market, an iPhone into everyone's hands? Can you imagine Southwest Airlines not funding operating expenses? Dan Pallotta, a fundraising activist and author of *Charity Case* and *Uncharitable*, urges that if we are going to build a more humane and positive future, a "new" way of helping organizations achieve their mission is a must. He, too, is on a crusade to help funders and organizations understand that operating expenses and sustainable funding are critical issues and that starving nonprofits so they do not have access to marketing dollars and the operating expenses they need to fully function is a recipe for disaster.

Our Call to Action

We invite nonprofits that want to change how they fund their mission and are determined to build their sustainability so they may continue to do good and fulfill their mission to explore with us how social enterprise can be a viable alternative to the ever-existing challenge of doing more with less. Our research and hands-on work with hundreds of nonprofit organizations, including our own, has given us some unique insights.

> What we are talking about in this manual is not theory. It is practical. It is useful. It is proven to work!

important

Our work is not theory. It takes starving nonprofits into sustainability. We think it's time to say, "I'm mad as heck, and I'm not going to take it anymore," and break out of the subsistence mindset into viability and sustainability and a future over which you have some control.

We passionately believe social enterprise is a way of stopping the cycle of:

◆ just one more ask (for money);

◆ just one more fundraising event;

◆ keeping your fingers crossed with breath held; and

◆ endless waiting for the yes or no answer and putting your head down with each rejection.

Social enterprise is a unique model for "doing business for the common good" while continuing to make the world a better place.

As a reminder, social enterprise is not for everyone. It is always about fulfilling the mission, which must rest on financial sustainability, a critical balancing proposition.

Join us on this journey of discovery to explore the way social enterprise may help your organization continue to do good with the resources you need every day. Each chapter in this manual will give you solid how-tos that will guide you each step of the way. We look forward to helping you and your organization build a stronger financial foundation that will help make the world a better, more vibrant community.

To Recap

◆ Economic changes, too few dollars, and expanding social needs have changed the traditional philanthropy model.

◆ Social enterprise helps organizations meet their mission using business models and earned revenue strategies.

◆ Social enterprises build sustainability through a diversified portfolio of revenue strategies not dependent on charity.

◆ Social enterprise ventures are growing, and funders are demanding measurable outcomes. It's time to pay attention to the triple bottom line of people, planet, and profits, not just the first two.

Chapter Two

Paradigm Shifts: The Business of Doing Good

IN THIS CHAPTER

- ···➔ Social enterprise is the business of doing good

- ···➔ Social enterprise uses business methods

- ···➔ There are established legal entities and structures that must be followed

- ···➔ Getting legal and financial advice is critical

Social enterprises have made significant gains in the last several years and are becoming an accepted part of the landscape as the economy and diminishing resources cause many nonprofits to examine how they are fulfilling their mission.

Finding the Right-for-You Enterprise

Often, social enterprises combine business and nonbusiness objectives within a single operation. How you will be capitalized or funded may be the deciding factor on how you form your enterprise.

There are several models that are appropriate for social enterprise ventures. Finding the right one may well be one of your biggest challenges. New business structures have emerged in the last several years that link profit ventures with nonprofits. The new structures range from low-profit limited liability companies to integrated structures and L3Cs, benefit corporations, and other hybrids in between. There are many choices, from being a for-profit corporation or a 501(c)(3) tax-exempt organization. Social enterprises can be formed as traditional businesses, socially responsible businesses, and traditional nonprofit or nongovernmental organizations.

> There are many types of business structures and options that can support your social enterprise. As you progress in the process from idea generation to formal structure, you should get professional advice as to which will best serve your social enterprise and your current nonprofit status.
>
> **observation**

With each model, there are issues and challenges that must be carefully examined beforehand, from enterprise design to governance, funding, taxation, and statutory and regulatory compliance. How you fund the enterprise will also be determined in part by your structure. You will need to review your potential options with a lawyer or CPA with nonprofit expertise. Do it now. You will need that expertise from the very beginning.

The LLC Option

If you require seed money or start-up capital, if it is coming from invested capital, and if your funders are expecting a financial return, then a business entity or limited liability company (LLC) may be your best bet. LLC laws generally allow for greater flexibility, the structuring of governance, and how the enterprise is run.

In fact, having a business structure as the vehicle for your social enterprise has its benefits. It gives you greater flexibility in raising capital, and it allows you to issue shares and pay dividends, avoid unrelated business income tax (UBIT), and partner in other profit-sharing ventures and arrangements with other businesses. Also keep in mind that the leaders of a for-profit business have a fiduciary responsibility to run the business in the best interests of its shareholders. Profit is a key consideration, not necessarily the organization's mission. Contributions are not tax deductible, nor can the business deduct more than 10 percent of its net income, which may limit what you want to accomplish for the mission of your organization.

The Nonprofit Option

If the seed funding or start-up capital funding for your enterprise is from donated money and no financial return is expected by your funders, then operating your enterprise within your nonprofit may be best. Nonprofits can't issue shares or distribute earnings or profits to investors. Still, a nonprofit provides a tax deduction for contributions. Nonprofits can issue debt and pay interest, but this is another one of those points you'd best get professional legal or accounting guidance on.

Unrelated Business Income Tax

Another area to be aware of is what is known as unrelated business income tax, or UBIT.

UBIT is not a mystery, a drawback, or anything to fear. UBIT is a tax on income a nonprofit may generate from "unrelated" business activities. If income is generated that does not contribute to the mission and purpose in any significant way other than make the organization money, then that income could be taxed at normal corporate rates. There are exceptions to this taxable income, such as the resale of donated items (as in a thrift shop) or an enterprise run primarily by volunteers, so review IRS publications and get professional tax advice as part of your research into the best model for your enterprise. Later in this manual, we'll delve deeper into this issue.

Pitfalls, Perils, and Paradoxes

Count on it. There are going to be challenges on your path to forming a social enterprise. Our purpose in this manual is to guide you through the process of research and feasibility, which is required to launch a successful social enterprise, not to advise, counsel, or provide legal advice on how to structure your social enterprise. That is very much outside the scope of this manual. However, we want to briefly review what you need to be more aware of so you can raise questions when working with your nonprofit attorney and CPA.

It is important to your success in social enterprise that you grasp a basic understanding of the business structural options and tax implications that might apply to your enterprise. While we can't give you the answers, we hope to inform you about the important questions you should ask your professional advisors.

 practical tip

Social enterprise, while it is a "business" activity dedicated to achieving a social goal that makes the world a better place, is not primarily motivated by profit for the sake of profit. Yet—and a big "yet" it is—while profit motives may be secondary, financial viability and sustainability absolutely require positive financial performance. To achieve success, it is imperative that a social enterprise look at market-based strategies so it can achieve the ultimate goal of doing good. And, readers, you must do well financially in order to go from charity to sustainability.

Once you get past the euphoria of "Wouldn't it be great to solve all of our problems by launching a social enterprise?" and the light bulbs stop blinking, sit down, pen and associates nearby, and ask some practical questions:

♦ Why is social enterprise a great idea for us?

♦ What do we really hope to accomplish? More mission? More money?

♦ Do we have a solid baseline from which to work to leverage our idea?

♦ What resources are we going to need?

♦ What don't we know, and how do we know what we don't know?

The following chapters will provide step-by-step guides and worksheets to help you ask even more critical questions on how to find the answers that can result in a viable social enterprise for your organization.

While a social enterprise directly supports social needs, usually by providing products or services, it is also about earned income strategies that produce revenue from the sale of

> To launch a successful social enterprise requires a group of committed individuals, staff, volunteers, and board members who are living and breathing social impact and applying business thinking, strategic planning, and management tools to the goal of doing good.

important

goods and services. This requires new thinking. It's not about donations, contributions, and special events. The problems nonprofits like yours have addressed for years are expanding. To be successful, social enterprise requires an entrepreneurial spirit, creative thinking, and a mindset that is capable of generating income streams that lead to sustainability.

It's a given that you're a great organization with terrific people or you wouldn't be wondering how you could do even more good, but we're now talking about the *business* of doing good. This involves a group of committed individuals, staff, volunteers, and board members who are living and breathing social impact and also applying business thinking, strategic planning, and management tools to reach the goals and objectives of your mission.

Be Aware of the Legal Issues

Maybe you are already doing this. However, in our experience, many nonprofits are presently ill equipped to begin a social enterprise. Serious questions need to be asked, many of which we will address in later chapters. Briefly, let's review the legal considerations.

Our advice, at the risk of repeating ourselves, is to make sure you consult an attorney and CPA with nonprofit expertise. The myriad complications of setting up the right entity are a critical part of your social enterprise planning and cannot be overemphasized. This is an area of expertise you can't leave to chance or the wrong people. Up-to-date knowledge about tax laws and entity formation so you stay on the good side of the IRS is critical.

Dream with your feet moving, not just your heart. Social enterprise has moved into the mainstream, investors are becoming more interested, and even the government has awakened to the possibilities. There is an eroding gulf between nonprofits and for-profits and sometimes there is an interlocking relationship with a for-profit organization that may be a parent subsidiary.

The complex legal liabilities, funding challenges, and governance all play a role in how you will set up your social enterprise. The best model for your enterprise is a key question around which many of your future decisions will be made. Learn more about the alternatives before you leap.

It is important that you clearly define your short-term and long-term desired outcomes. The kind of enterprise you are launching may well determine the entity you establish.

Success Means Being Well Capitalized

You must do well to do good. If you don't have money, you can't fulfill your mission, no matter how high your hopes or how much good you accomplish. Good equals value. Whether you decide that your social enterprise will be established as a for-profit business or a part of your nonprofit exempt organization, "not profitable" is not an option. This means being well capitalized. You can't run a business without money, and cash is still king. If you're not profitable, you'll keep relying entirely on the old models of funding that led you to an interest in social enterprise to begin with. If you want to change the world, you need the funds to do it, end of story. And this may be your biggest obstacle, developing a financial mindset and having enterprise team members who will be your advocates and advisors and still be tough when needed.

Develop your financial literacy. You might not be the numbers person, but someone on your team needs to understand profit, ROI, ROA, taxes, investing, and the dynamics of raising capital. Be brutally honest as part of the process of establishing your social enterprise.

> We repeat, you must do well to do good. If you don't have money, you can't fulfill your mission, no matter how high your hopes or how important your mission is. "Not profitable" is not an option. You can't run a business without money, and cash is still king. It is not okay to not be sustainable.

important

While not every social enterprise requires capital investment, as part of your planning, you'll need to ask yourself if you have the capital you need to start your enterprise. If you don't have it, do you know where to get capital if you need it? Do you know how to present a case for capital investment? Start with this as a strong possibility: You may need seed money or a capital investment. You need to know about credits and debits, how to read financial statements, and the joys of budgeting, not budgeting for a traditional grant but budgeting from a business standpoint.

Running Your Organization Like a Business

There is a myth about what tax-exempt organizations can and cannot do we'd like to dispel: "Nonprofits cannot be run like businesses." Originally attributed to Jim Collins, the author of *Good to Great and the Social Sectors*, in an invitation to subscribe to *Nonprofit Quarterly*, he supposedly said, "We must reject the idea—well intentioned but dead wrong—that the primary path to greatness in the social sectors is to become more like a business." The quote, which was taken out of context, has halted many an organization. We challenge you to think that if your nonprofit organization embraces this theory, you may not truly understand that just like a for-profit business, you too must be a sustainable entity and be fiscally flourishing. For your nonprofit to serve its mission, you must realize that you are a business. You do yourselves an injustice if you think otherwise. If there is no money, if your nonprofit continually operates in the red, it will cease to do good and will be out of business.

> *You don't make a business profitable by having for-profit tax status, and you can't operate a business if it is unprofitable, even if it has nonprofit tax status.*
>
> Clara Miller
> Nonprofit Finance Fund

So, what does it mean to operate like a business?

Consider your value. A for-profit or nonprofit has a service or product that people value or not. What do you offer that people will value? Traditionally, many nonprofits have not been effective at demonstrating the value of their services, much less articulating that value so clients are interested enough to engage their services or buy their products.

In a for-profit business, that value is determined by profit. In a nonprofit, donors contribute to the nonprofit that exemplifies and enhances the beliefs they respect and personally value. In the case of a social enterprise, asking what you have of value that will generate revenue to support the mission of your organization needs some thought.

There is also a myth that ROI, or return on investment, has no place in a nonprofit. ROI is a measure of the net income an organization's management is able to earn with its total assets. It is calculated by dividing net profits (after taxes if applicable) by total assets. ROI is sometimes referred to as rate of return or return on assets. This is especially important if one partners with a corporation. In fact, many donors are investing in charitable organizations. They expect to see an impact, measurable outcomes, and demonstrated track records of effectiveness. And, once again, if your nonprofit is not making money, it will cease to exist.

The Art and Science of Business Plans

So, what goes into a well-thought-out, artfully crafted business plan (which we will help you design in a later chapter)?

Let's just look at the basics.

The actual process and methodology for developing a business plan gives you a road map for discussing your hopes, dreams, and aspirations. It gives you a forum for communication and dialogue that builds excitement and momentum with the internal team and any stakeholders you may include. This dialogue is where the vision of the enterprise is expressed so that your story can be communicated to all stakeholders.

observation

A business plan is the document that represents who you are, what you value, and how you will give value. It defines your organization and the results you will accomplish—the who, what, where, when, and why. It's also a road map that guides your organization and a tool to inform others of your intentions. Putting together a business plan requires thoroughness and patience. If you need capital for your social enterprise, the business plan is your definitive document. It is your guide for getting there, wherever "there" is. It provides benchmarks for financial profit and sustainability.

Most of us are not experienced business plan writers. This may be one of those areas that requires the help and advice of an outside professional who knows how to put together and articulate the vision of your enterprise so that potential investors and stakeholders are excited and eager to support your enterprise. Your business plan allows staff and volunteers to clearly see the direction of the enterprise, and management has a guideline to follow. It requires a knowledge of the numbers that create the critical financial picture and analysis investors require. Building a business plan is not for the timid.

However, a business plan is essential, so bite the bullet and be prepared to condense everything you've learned about beginning a successful social enterprise into a concise business plan. You're going to need a plan to inspire and focus the troops and yourself. Don't struggle with this issue. If you'll carefully follow the steps in the upcoming chapters, you'll learn everything you'll need to create a viable and useful business plan. In fact, we'll even give you a template, and there are many good examples of social enterprise business plans available on the Internet. See **Appendix A** in this manual for the draft of a business plan developed by a graduate of our social enterprise training program.

> The important thing to remember is this: A business plan without thorough feasibility studies is an empty plan.
>
>
> important

Why a Business Plan Is Important

Putting together your business plan from conception to completion forces you to take a critical objective look at your entire business concept from beginning to end.

Your business plan is an operating tool that serves as a guideline for managing your enterprise and working toward your goals and ultimate success.

Your business plan is the communication tool for those who may provide funding or other resources. This is what you will use for engaging with funders, investors, and bankers if you require start-up investment.

Your plan is the basis for how to run your social enterprise and serves as a guide for what the management team, staff, and volunteers intend to achieve.

Your business plan will serve as the framework for your marketing and sales plans, pricing, distribution, advertising, social media, and staffing models.

Your business plan keeps you centered on the end result. It gives you a means for staying focused and checking on your progress.

Leadership

No, it's not deliberately last on the list because it's the least important challenge in launching a successful social enterprise. Quite the contrary.

In fact, leadership could easily be the first issue you deal with. Do you have the right leadership in place? Does your leadership team of staff and board have an entrepreneurial mindset? Does your staff have any business experience? Taking the organization to a more entrepreneurial level means both staff and board leadership may require a different set of skills. As you work through this manual, you will identify the specific skills that will be required for your social enterprise. You can include in your plan how you will recruit, hire, or contract those skills if they do not currently exist in your organization.

Do you have the right leadership at the board and staff levels to lead the process to form a successful social enterprise? Does your staff have the required business skills to run a social enterprise? Launching and running a social enterprise requires a different set of skills and tools from those required to operate your traditional nonprofit programs and services.

important

Are you still with us? So far, this probably sounds like a lot of work. And you're right. It is.

Establishing a social enterprise is challenging. There are issues you have to examine and plan for so they don't become insurmountable obstacles. Planning for and establishing a successful business—and, yes, we are talking "business"—means having the foresight to start off on the right foot from the very beginning.

Now let's start the rest of your journey, putting it all to work, one step at a time.

Come with us for the rest of this expedition.

To Recap

◆ Social enterprise generates unrestricted revenue streams and additional resources that build sustainability.

◆ Social enterprise uses business activities and methods to meet your mission, yet is not primarily motivated by profit.

◆ There are numerous venues for establishing your social enterprise, each with its own set of rules and advantages.

◆ Getting sound legal and financial advice from those with nonprofit expertise from the very beginning is essential to sort through the options and complexity.

Chapter Three

Vetting the Social Enterprise Model

IN THIS CHAPTER

··→ The difference between traditional funding and social enterprise

··→ What is required to become a successful social entrepreneur?

··→ How long will it take?

··→ Myths about social enterprise

··→ What can you expect from this process?

The funding marketplace has changed over the past few years. Much of corporate giving is being redirected toward *investing* rather than buying tables for galas, which are on the decline in many markets. Government funding is diminishing, while traditional funding sources are less and less reliable. Successful businesses and donors are tired of giving to organizations that operate with the mentality that they will be continually bailed out by someone else.

What does this change in the funding marketplace mean for your organization? It means a shift to earned income instead of relying on a handout.

How prepared is your organization to endure these changes in the marketplace? Have you created a plan to diversify your income streams? Is your organization working strategically toward financial self-sustainability?

The Difference Between Traditional Funding and Earned Income

Traditional funding is familiar to most nonprofit organizations. It includes grants, special events, donations, sponsorships, underwriting, annual campaigns, and all the things we've been doing in the nonprofit sector for years to generate more funding. You work hard to get the money, you use it up, and then you have to go back—often to the same sources—to get more. Inevitably, there are strings attached to this money. Grantors place restrictions upon the use of their grant money and require reports to ensure that you have met their funding requirements.

> Realize that nonprofit is a tax designation, not a business plan. Nobody is *requiring* you to lose money.
>
> **food for thought**

Donors, too, have expectations. Even with a special event, donors expect to have a good time, enjoy the food, be recognized, etc. This could also be considered restricted money.

Earned income, or *social enterprise*, is simply money that *you* have generated through product sales, payment for services, or other business opportunities. It is *yours to use as your organization sees fit*. When it is successful, it builds upon itself and earns more. It is *unrestricted income* that creates the path toward self-sustainability and enhances your mission.

What Is Required to Become a Successful Social Entrepreneur?

Successful entrepreneurial nonprofits embrace the big picture. They think and act strategically. They build plans. They educate themselves about market trends, customer buying cycles, and consumer benefits, and they know their competition. Successful social entrepreneurs "Get Up and Get Out" to test their assumptions. Most important of all, successful social entrepreneurs invest their resources to grow and enhance their mission.

It Takes a Team

A dedicated team of board members, staff, and others should participate in the hands-on tasks in this workbook. At least eight to twelve dedicated team members is probably required for this effort. We have actually worked with teams as large as thirty, however. Fewer than four or five team members could make the process more difficult, as there are fewer members to do the work required in addition to their regular day-to-day responsibilities. Your team should include representatives from all levels in your organization to take advantage of their diverse perspectives and to generate ownership. You might also consider including entrepreneurs from the community as advisors.

> Giving this manual to one person to complete won't work. It takes a dedicated team to participate in the social enterprise process.
>
> **important**

Why does it take a team? Think of it this way. We've all been to a workshop or a conference and then returned to work all fired up with new ideas, new enthusiasm, new energy—and been told to sit down, take it easy, and not rock the boat. One person alone can't create the process for internal systemic change that is required to launch a successful social enterprise. You simply cannot do it alone.

Why is it critical to include board members on the team? What happens if the staff gets ahead of the board? Yes, indeed, it is likely that the reins will get yanked and the progress for change will be delayed while the board gets brought up to speed and understands what is going on inside the organization it governs.

So build a team of diverse board and staff members. Make sure every member of the team is committed to the journey.

Define roles and expectations for all members of your team. Embrace diversity of opinions. You'll also discover an additional benefit of this process—working together in a new and purposeful manner will dramatically enhance your organization's teamwork. And we promise you that adopting many of the skills required to launch a successful social enterprise will also increase your organizational efficiency and effectiveness.

We want to remind you that this process is complex and time consuming but incredibly important to the future of your organization.

Some who read this manual and use it as a guide will reap the benefits and will be able to launch a successful social enterprise in a few months. Others will discover that the time, staff, and resources required to work through the manual will require outside help to keep them on track. We've been there, done it, and understand this, so don't be afraid to ask for help along the way.

Myths About Social Enterprise

Let's get some of the common myths about social enterprise out of the way right now so you can open your mind to the possibilities of sustainability through earned income.

Myth Number One: Nonprofits Can't Make a Profit

Of course you can! You are now. You just aren't paying taxes on it. That's the whole point of fundraising, isn't it? Generating revenue to accomplish the mission. An easily recognized example is Girl Scout Cookies. The girls develop business and social skills, and the organization earns unrestricted revenue.

Myth Number Two: If We Earn Money, We'll Lose Our Tax-Exempt Status

This is not likely. At the current time, the IRS states that until earned revenue becomes a significant portion of your annual income, or if generating earned income requires a significant portion of your resources, your tax-exempt status is not at risk. Way before (or if) your tax-exempt status is at risk, however, there are numerous ways to protect your status as a nonprofit entity, including spinning off the enterprise into a for-profit whose profit supports the nonprofit's mission. Don't worry about that yet. Even if you would need to, there is plenty of time to get the advice of nonprofit legal and accounting professionals to help you manage this.

Myth Number Three: Oh No, We'll Have to Pay Tax!

Maybe you will. Maybe you won't. But what *if* your enterprise is taxable? We'll discuss the possibility of unrelated business income tax (UBIT) in **Chapter Eight**. Our advice is simple: Build it into the cost of doing business and pay the tax. In fact, you might discover that paying tax on your earned income removes objections from a for-profit entity with which you might compete.

Myth Number Four: It's a Quick Fix

All right! We'll just read this manual and be ready to start a social enterprise. Not so fast! Think of this simple example. Let's say that someone in your office makes great egg salad sandwiches, so you decide to sell them as a social enterprise. Do you run to the store, buy lots of bread, eggs, and mayonnaise, make a bunch of sandwiches, and start selling them on the corner by your office? Of course not! Intuitively, you know there are many questions that need to be answered and regulations to be addressed, such as licensing for sales, rules about food storage and packaging, questions about the best place for your sales booth, deciding on a price, knowing how many sandwiches to make, knowing your competition, asking whether customers want sandwiches delivered or if they'll even buy egg salad sandwiches, etc., etc., etc.

Of course, you would answer these questions and more before you bought bread and eggs. The same is true for starting your social enterprise. This manual will guide you through the process so you can start successfully. However, some words of caution. The process to go from idea to enterprise is not easy or quick, and it is entirely possible that your organization will require professional help along the way.

> Social enterprise is *not* about turning your nonprofit into a business. It *is* about applying sound business principles to your tax-exempt business.
>
> **principle**

How Long Will the Social Enterprise Process Take?

You've probably read statistics about the amount of time it takes to build a successful business, the average being three to five years. The same could be said for launching a successful social enterprise. Some organizations we have advised have been ready to launch within several months and realize a profit almost immediately. Often it takes longer, depending upon the size and scope of the business venture and the current status of the nonprofit's organization and dynamics.

The actual process described in this manual could take from three to nine months, or even longer, depending upon the size and scope of your social enterprise idea. It is important to keep the egg salad sandwich business in mind when you think about this process. If you short-cut the steps, you could risk putting your valuable organizational assets at risk.

What You Can Expect as a Result of This Process

There are many benefits to be realized as a result of embedding the social enterprise process into how you run your nonprofit organization, including:

◆ Fundamental and systemic changes in the way you manage your nonprofit business. Merely applying sound business principles to how you manage your everyday nonprofit business will reap untold benefits. You'll think differently about your organization, realizing a shift from *charity-think* to *business-think*. You'll recognize the real value of what you do, what you have, and what you know.

◆ A business plan for an earned income social enterprise venture. Your business plan will be based on sound market research and feasibility, not on assumptions and wishful thinking.

◆ Refinement and enhancement of your current programs and services. Many organizations that go through the process described in this manual choose not to start new enterprises after all. Rather, they provide value-added benefits to current programs and services that create new income sources targeted at current or new clients/customers, either nonprofit or for-profit. The process itself allows you to look at ways to streamline and be more effective and efficient.

> Social service providers often find themselves promoted to management levels within their nonprofit organizations. Nonprofit managers enthusiastically excel in their areas of expertise—managing people and program service protocols. Managing budgets is much tougher, especially when one needs to raise matching funds to replace shrinking grant dollars. Social enterprise was the answer for our agency.
>
> J. Copeland

◆ A new language and a new objective method by which to evaluate current and future programs, services, and income opportunities. How will you decide whether an enterprise idea is likely to work? We'll show you how to develop an objective decision-making tool you can adapt to help make sound objective decisions about new programs and services, fundraising ideas, and more.

◆ At the core, completing this journey will result in fundamental organizational changes to support your mission. This can be a powerful process that offers many benefits beyond the creation of a successful social enterprise.

So get ready for an exciting journey!

To Recap

◆ It takes a team of dedicated staff and volunteers to complete the social enterprise process successfully.

◆ It takes time to do it right. Launching a social enterprise is not a quick fix.

◆ Don't get lost in the typical myths about social enterprise.

◆ In addition to generating unrestricted revenue, you can expect systemic changes in the way you operate your tax-exempt business.

Chapter Four

Organizational Goals, Focus, and Desired Outcomes

IN THIS CHAPTER

···→ Internal and external forces

···→ Desired outcomes

···→ Your vision and mission

···→ Stakeholder communication plan

···→ Worksheets one through eight

The social enterprise process will test and challenge many of your assumptions about your organization—who you are and who you aren't, what you know and what you don't, why you exist, who you serve, and so much more.

We believe that for this process to be successfully integrated within your organization, it must be based on a thorough knowledge and *collective* understanding of the basics. If individual members of your team start from different perspectives, it is unlikely that you will reach a successful conclusion and you'll have wasted valuable resources along the way. Equally important is consensus on the reasons you have embarked on the road to social enterprise to begin with and what you expect to gain from it.

Use the worksheets in this manual to stimulate and enhance teamwork and to build consensus. Use them as they are presented, or modify them for your purposes. Remember, it takes a dedicated team to do this work.

Let's start with the basics: clarifying what has brought you to attempt this social enterprise process and what you expect to gain from the journey.

Why is this an important place to start? Well, not everyone is excited and challenged by the process of change, and your team will need to provide clear, concise, and consistent messages as you proceed.

The following initial exercises will help your team clarify its focus. You may find it more difficult than you think to gain consensus, but it is critical that all members of the team agree before moving to the next phase. So spend the time required to get everyone on the same page before you move to the next step.

One way to gain the most benefit from these exercises is to ask each member of your team to complete the exercise independently, then reconvene, share, discuss, and gain consensus. We also suggest that you might want to share these exercises with others in your organization to enhance clarity and focus.

Internal and External Forces

The social enterprise process will change much about how your organization operates in the future. Change is not always embraced with enthusiasm by all, especially those who may not have been directly involved in working through this manual and who are wondering what all this change is about, why it's occurring, and how it will impact them. The obvious result could be negativity and a stubborn reluctance to embrace the social enterprise ideas.

It is critical that your team be united and clear about the reasons you've embarked upon this social enterprise process and why change is required.

Once again, our best advice it to have every member of the team complete these exercises, then come together to share and gain consensus.

Worksheet One: Internal and External Forces

Internal forces might include the need to expand services, hire additional staff, or improve staff salaries or benefits. Be specific!

Internal forces requiring us to change:

◆ _____

◆ _____

◆ _____

◆ _____

External forces might include a current or anticipated reduction in funding, competition from other organizations, federal or local legislative changes. Be specific!

External forces requiring us to change:

◆ _____

◆ _____

◆ _____

◆ _____

Desired Outcomes

Here again, it is important to be very clear about what you expect to gain from your social enterprise. You should set both mission-based goals and money-based goals. These goals should be clear and measurable. They will be critical as you move along the social enterprise journey, because you will want to check back regularly to see if your proposed social enterprise will lead you to achieve your stated goals.

Worksheet Two: Mission Goals

How will you enhance your mission with additional unrestricted revenue?

Examples

Review these examples of mission goals to get you started.

◆ Increase the number of clients served by 25 percent within five years (total 136 new clients).

◆ Develop new programs to serve unmet markets within three years, e.g., serve elderly in the north sector.

◆ Provide financial assistance to fifty additional families within two years.

Identify up to three mission goals. Be specific. Ensure they are measurable. Work independently first. Gain the consensus of the entire enterprise team.

1. _____

2. _____

3. _____

Worksheet Three: Financial Goals

Estimate how much it will cost to meet your mission goals.

Examples

Review these examples of financial goals to get you started.

- ◆ Achieve 25 percent of annual budget from earned income ($125,000) within five years.

- ◆ Replace lost grant income of $80,000 within three years.

- ◆ Generate $75,000 in unrestricted net revenue within two years.

Identify up to three financial goals. Be specific. Ensure they are measurable. Work independently first. Gain the consensus of the entire enterprise team.

1. _____

2. _____

3. _____

Your Vision

Now let's expand your thinking. An important exercise for your team is to think ahead to visualize how your organization will be different in the future as a result of this social enterprise process. A vision statement should be broad and far reaching. It should describe how things would look if you were able to solve problems, change the world, improve the environment, or whatever the ultimate goal is.

A vision statement does not state *how* this will be accomplished. Rather, it defines a better or different universe. It is not so important that this vision is ever achieved. Instead, think of it as the reason you serve. This is a powerful exercise—and one to consider revisiting each year as part of your organization's strategic planning process. It helps gets everyone on the same page and creates a hopeful framework for board, staff, and volunteers in which to do their important work.

Your organizational vision is a key component in the development of your social enterprise. Clearly, your enterprise should support your vision of the future.

Examples of Vision Statements

Review these examples of vision statements to get you started.

- ◆ We live in a world free of violence and oppression. (A domestic violence shelter)

◆ Every human is treated with dignity and respect, regardless of disabilities. (An agency serving the developmentally disabled)

◆ All animals are loved and cherished by the humans with whom they coexist. (An animal shelter)

◆ Every child receives a well-rounded education, regardless of socioeconomic status. (An agency serving low-income and disadvantaged children)

Worksheet Four: Vision Statement

Bring your social enterprise planning team together for deep discussions about *why* you exist and what you expect to achieve in the future. Gain consensus about this critical beginning step in the process of change through social enterprise.

Our Vision Statement

_____

_____

_____

_____

_____

Your Mission

A clear and simple mission statement should explain *what* you do and *how* you will achieve your organization's vision. The mission statement should serve as a guide for your organization's day-to-day operation and strategic planning. Everything you do should fit within the confines of your mission statement. You will want to check your current mission statement to see if it fits your organization's vision. If not, this is a great time to craft a better version.

Examples of Mission Statements

Review these examples of mission statements to get you started. Notice how they support the vision statements above.

◆ To shelter and empower survivors of intimate partner domestic violence and to improve the way [the state] responds to this violence. (A shelter for victims of domestic violence)

◆ Working together to open doors for people with developmental disabilities to be valued members of the community. (An agency serving the developmentally disabled)

◆ To improve the lives of companion animals through sheltering, adoption, community education, providing quality veterinary services to families in need, and programs that reduce pet overpopulation. (An animal shelter)

◆ To promote the school readiness of children ages birth to five from low-income families by enhancing their cognitive, social, and emotional development. (An agency serving low income and disadvantaged children)

Worksheet Five: Mission Statement

Our Mission Statement

Does it explain how you will achieve your vision?

_____

_____

_____

_____

_____

Core Values

Now it's time to create another crucial benchmark in the social enterprise process. You don't ever want to be tempted to start an earned income venture that could challenge or betray your organization's core values. Core values are those defining principles and values that hold your organization true to its vision and mission. Core values are like a plumb bob or directional compass that keeps you pointed true north.

> You should never be tempted to endorse an idea for earned income that won't serve your mission and vision or that betrays your core values. These three things will be critical and important benchmarks in your social enterprise process.

It is very important that all members of your organization share these core values and that you test your ideas for earned income to ensure that your core values are not betrayed. For example, if your mission is to reduce drug and alcohol abuse, would you endorse a social enterprise that sold alcoholic beverages at a coffee shop? You can see how this would be an important discussion to have to ensure all team members are in agreement before moving forward.

A frank discussion about your core values could be challenging. Nearly every nonprofit cites core values such as *integrity, respect, honesty,* and the like. But what do these values really *mean*? You probably have a list of values in a nice frame somewhere, but are they an integral part of your daily work? How do you define them in your day-to-day operations?

This is another important exercise that you might want to share with your organization's stakeholders: staff, volunteers, clients, etc. Your enterprise team could use this exercise to introduce the concepts of social enterprise and the goals you have set for the social enterprise process.

Worksheet Six: Core Values

Our Core Values

◆ _____

◆ _____

◆ _____

◆ _____

◆ _____

◆ _____

◆ _____

◆ _____

◆ _____

◆ _____

◆ _____

◆ _____

Organizational Stakeholders

We referred to your organization's stakeholders earlier in this chapter. As you embark on this social enterprise process, it is critical that you involve all types of organizational stakeholders in the process and apprise them of your progress. Not only will stakeholders have valuable insights and opinions, but they are likely to resist if they are not kept informed.

Consider these stakeholders and their potential concerns. What would threaten them if change were to occur? Discuss this with your team. Add other concerns you can identify.

Consider this: Your social enterprise team goes off to special meetings, comes back energized, has more meetings, speaks in a different language, and appears to have the inside track on what is happening in your organization. Staff members who are excluded from the process will surely feel left out, become suspicious and resentful, and resist the changes that are likely to come. The NIMBY (not in my backyard) effect will blossom like a weed, spread, and stymie progress.

observation

Worksheet Seven: Organizational Stakeholders

Stakeholder	Potential Concerns
Board members	◆ Will we stray from our mission? ◆ What effect will this have on our budget? ◆ What will the public think about this? ◆ _____ ◆ _____ ◆ _____
Staff	◆ Will we stray from our mission? ◆ What will this do to my department? ◆ How will this affect my job? ◆ Will I lose control? ◆ _____ ◆ _____ ◆ _____
Volunteers	◆ Will we stray from our mission? ◆ What effect will this have on me? ◆ _____ ◆ _____ ◆ _____
Clients	◆ Will I have to pay more for services? ◆ Will you reduce services? ◆ _____ ◆ _____ ◆ _____
Funders/donors	◆ Will you stray from your mission? ◆ Will this still require our support? ◆ What will be different? ◆ _____ ◆ _____ ◆ _____
General public	◆ Will you stray from your mission? ◆ What will you do differently? ◆ Will you still be a nonprofit? ◆ _____ ◆ _____ ◆ _____
Other (identify)	◆ _____ ◆ _____ ◆ _____ ◆ _____ ◆ _____ ◆ _____

Stakeholder Communication Plan

Now that you have identified some of the potential concerns of your stakeholders, it's time to undertake some simple market research. Assign team members to speak to representatives of each stakeholder group. Explain what you are doing (social enterprise) and why you are doing it (external and internal forces, mission, and dollar goals). Ask about their concerns, how they'd like to be kept informed, what suggestions they may have, and if they want to participate.

You will need to reach consensus about your team's responses so you deliver a consistent message about the social enterprise process. Take a few minutes to discuss your team's response to each of your organization's main stakeholders. Refer to the results of your stakeholder market research. Then draft a plan using the next worksheet that will formalize how and when you will communicate with each stakeholder group. Consider regular meetings, surveys, open forums, emails, and other communication opportunities.

Why is a stakeholder communication plan important? Here's an example: The chief executive of a fairly large organization had carefully selected the members of her social enterprise team. The team began by asking other staff for input and suggestions but failed to follow up with regular updates and information. The result? A mutiny! Fearful of the changes to occur, the rest of the staff dug in their heels, refused to be supportive, and undermined the work of the social enterprise team. The mutiny had to be overturned by an outside consultant (one of the authors of this manual) before the work could continue.

 stories from the real world

Worksheet Eight: Stakeholder Communication Plan

Stakeholder	Primary Concern(s)	Message(s)	Plan
Board			
Staff			

Stakeholder	Primary Concern(s)	Message(s)	Plan
Volunteers			
Clients			
Funders/donors			
General public			
Other (identify)			

To Recap

◆ Laying the groundwork and gaining consensus from your enterprise team is the critical first step in the social enterprise process.

◆ Benchmarks include driving forces, mission, and dollar goals.

◆ All enterprise team members must agree about your organization's vision, mission, and core values.

◆ Stakeholders can make or break the social enterprise process. A stakeholder communication plan helps them understand and support the process.

Chapter Five

Examining Your Assets and Opportunities—What You Do, What You Have, What You Know

IN THIS CHAPTER

- ···→ Create an asset inventory

- ···→ Establish objective decision-making criteria

- ···→ Brainstorm social enterprise opportunities

- ···→ Select "The Big Idea"

- ···→ Worksheets nine through twelve

Now that you have set mission and financial outcomes and have clarified your vision, mission, and core values, it is time to identify potential social enterprise ideas and narrow the focus to one or two of these that you believe at this point will best meet your goals. It is important to narrow the field of potential ideas so you can focus and complete rigorous market research and feasibility studies that will prevent putting valuable organizational assets at risk.

We have learned by experience that it is usually best that your first social enterprise be based on something you currently do, currently have, or currently know. It leverages your experience and can reduce risk.

At this point, perhaps the largest limitation nonprofits place on themselves in the social enterprise process is to *undervalue* their assets. Don't let this happen to you! Change your thinking to understand that what you do every day (and probably take for granted) *is* rocket science to someone who doesn't do it or know it. Your assets are valuable. Don't underestimate yourself.

This next step in the process will guide you to develop a comprehensive list of your organizational assets. This isn't as easy as you may think. You will use this list as a springboard to brainstorm about how you can leverage your assets into earned revenue, so you must break every asset down into its smallest parts. For example, don't just list "training" as an asset. What kind of training? What do you have to know to deliver the training? What skills and knowledge are required? What is delivered in the training? Who is trained? Who could it benefit? We are looking here for details, details, and more details.

Consider all that is involved in providing child care, as another example. There are numerous technical, knowledge, and physical assets required to provide for just one child.

> *This process changed our thinking. Free has turned to fee! Given this funding environment, we have taken some major hits, but we are growing our programs, we are not shrinking, and we are not laying off people. Our social enterprise is now a mature business and is really pumping out some money. If we hadn't done this, we would be in a heap of hurt.*
>
> Donna T.

Develop Your Asset Inventory

Start by listing your assets in the following categories:

1. *What You Do Extremely Well*—your core competencies. For example, an emergency response agency responds to disasters in two hours. That response could be considered its product or service. Core competencies include volunteer management, fleet management, communication, supplies management, safety training, emergency training, and much more, each of which should be broken down into smaller elements.

2. *What You Have*—your physical assets. For example, a community action agency has its offices in a large building, half of which is vacant. The vacant part of the building is an underutilized physical asset that could be leveraged into earned income. Consider things you have with excess capacity: land, buildings, vehicles, equipment. List each one separately, and be specific.

3. *What You Know*—your technical and knowledge assets. For example, the staff of a community theater could transfer its knowledge of makeup, costuming, set construction, design, and acting into other venues that earn income. Identify what you and your staff and volunteers know that others might want or need.

4. Finally, *Who You Know*—relationships that you can leverage. For example, business leaders, legal or accounting professionals with nonprofit expertise, those with experience in the type of enterprise you might start, investors or financers who can provide advice throughout the social enterprise process.

Complete the next worksheet to identify your assets. Share this worksheet with other stakeholders in your organization (staff, clients, volunteers) to gain their valuable input. You'll be surprised at all you do, all you have, and all you know!

Challenge: How many of these worksheets can you fill? Don't worry so much about getting the assets listed in the right category. Just create a comprehensive and detailed list of all your valuable assets.

Worksheet Nine: Make an Inventory of Your Assets

What We Are Good At (Core Competencies)	What We Have (Physical Assets)

What We Know (Knowledge Assets)	Who We Know (Relationship Assets)

Objective Criteria

As you were creating your asset inventory, we'll bet your team began to come up with some great ideas about how you might earn revenue. That's natural and is a fun part of this process.

However, before you can leap from assets to brainstorming potential earned income opportunities, you need to develop an objective method to evaluate these potential opportunities. It is far too easy to convince yourself that something is "The Big Idea" just because you fall in love with it! Instead, your mission and your valuable assets require that you develop a thorough and objective decision-making process.

The next step is to define the objective criteria that your team will use to evaluate all of the great ideas you will generate for earned income, based on leveraging your asset inventory.

You can use this objective method to evaluate not only potential earned income ideas but also your current programs and services. As a result, you might discover that some of your traditional fundraising and even current programs and services require a more careful evaluation to ensure their cost effectiveness, efficiency, and return on your investment of time and talent.

> Consider how an objective decision-making process can help evaluate ideas for new programs or services and fundraising opportunities as well as ideas for social enterprise. This is a tool you could include in your organizational tool kit to help with discussions and decisions in the future.
>
>  practical tip

We suggest that you develop a set of no more than eight to nine evaluation criteria. You may find this exercise more difficult than it looks to gain consensus from your enterprise team on what matters.

The criteria should be stated as sentences and must be definitive and measurable. Be sure to clarify and agree before your team accepts a criterion. Merely stating "will have minimal impact on current resources" is not clear. What resources (people? money? time?), and how will you define minimal?

Here are some examples of the types of objective criteria others have developed. You can use this as a starting point, but don't just accept this list. Discuss and define each one for *your* team and *your* organization. You will find that the discussion can be eye opening!

- ◆ Fits with mission, vision, and core values.

- ◆ Will have less than $_____ in start-up costs.

- ◆ Will have no impact on current staff.

- ◆ Won't detract from current programs and services.

◆ Will enhance agency image with stakeholders.

◆ Has income potential of $_____ within ____ years.

◆ Allows for collaboration with other agencies.

◆ Starts with something we already do, have, and know.

◆ Builds organizational capacity to deliver more services.

◆ Has demonstrated growth potential of _____ by _____.

◆ Is not dependent on volunteers.

◆ Has no initial capital investment.

And consider one of our favorites: It will be *fun*.

Worksheet Ten: Objective Criteria

Develop your objective criteria here. Remember to write your criteria as statements. Ensure agreement from your enterprise team before accepting a criterion.

1. _____

2. _____

3. _____

4. _____

5. _____

6. _____

7. _____

8. _____

9. _____

Brainstorm Opportunities

Now have fun!

Identify as many opportunities as you can for earned income through social enterprise.

Get your creative juices flowing and brainstorm about earned income opportunities. Start by reviewing your asset inventory. Then brainstorm how you might leverage your assets. Think of your assets as rocket science to someone who doesn't have it, know it, or do it. No idea is a bad idea at this stage in the journey. Don't make judgments. You'll use your objective criteria for sorting through these ideas later.

Don't undervalue your assets. Remember that what you do and know every day *is* rocket science to someone who doesn't do or know it!

Don't limit your brainstorming to easy ideas within the traditional nonprofit sector. Your rocket science could be sold to other nonprofits. Or to for-profit businesses. Or to a new and different client base. Or even to your current client base.

You might want to gather your ideas into categories such as:

1. *Service opportunity:* delivers a service directly to a market that you currently serve or one that you could serve—another nonprofit, a for-profit, or individuals. For example, a family service agency had listed several programs serving seniors that were spread throughout different departments. The agency developed a menu of services aimed at keeping seniors independent and formed a new and separate department with staff to manage it.

2. *Knowledge opportunity:* delivers a knowledge asset to a current or new market—another nonprofit, a for-profit, or individuals. For example, a faith-based counseling agency developed a continuing education program for medical professionals. A residential treatment agency opened its required employee safety training programs to other nonprofits and for-profit day care businesses for a fee. A community action agency modified its client-based financial literacy program and sold it to for-profit businesses as an employee benefit and a way for the business owner to reduce the costs incurred with dealing with employee financial illiteracy.

3. *Product opportunity:* produces or delivers a tangible product to another nonprofit, a for-profit, or individuals. For example, a food bank added nonfood items to its inventory, sold these to current food bank clients, and created a new market with nonfood nonprofits. A domestic violence center produced aromatic soaps and candles made by its residents, starting an Internet business.

4. Employment opportunity: provides direct employment to current or future clients or others. For example, an agency serving the disabled community expanded its sheltered workshop to provide new services, such as document shredding, shrink-wrap packaging, and bulk mailing. An agency training former felons in baking skills opened a bakery. An agency with back-to-work programs started a landscape business.

5. *Unrelated venture opportunity:* takes advantage of underutilized assets or develops an opportunity unrelated to your asset inventory. For example, an agency leveraged its relationships and brought its vehicle-donation program in house. In another example, an agency brought its facilities management in house, reducing high overhead costs.

> Collect your ideas for social enterprise in the following categories: service opportunity, knowledge opportunity, product opportunity, employment opportunity, and even unrelated venture opportunity. How many potential ideas can your team generate?
>
> **food for thought**

Worksheet Eleven: Brainstorm Opportunities

Don't stop with this worksheet! How many great ideas can you generate? Remember, in brainstorming, the sky's the limit. Your enterprise team can certainly share this brainstorming opportunity with those stakeholders you identified earlier to get their valuable input and get them excited about the social enterprise process.

1. _____
2. _____
3. _____
4. _____
5. _____
6. _____
7. _____
8. _____
9. _____
10. _____
11. _____
12. _____
13. _____
14. _____
15. _____
16. _____
17. _____
18. _____
19. _____
20. _____

Don't stop here! Fill more sheets with great ideas for social enterprise.

Evaluate Your Ideas

Now that you have brainstormed dozens of ideas for earned income through social enterprise, you have to narrow the list to one or two ideas that you think will attain your mission and dollar goals.

This is when those objective criteria you set in worksheet ten will become another valuable asset.

Here's how to use the next worksheet. Create a master document, listing all the great ideas your team generated in the left-hand column. Then list your objective criteria across the top. Distribute the worksheet to all team members, asking each to complete it independently. They should score the ideas from one to five, with one being the lowest to match a criterion, five the highest, and zero for "I don't know."

Then, in a meeting with all team members, share their individual rankings and discuss variances, coming to consensus on the one or two (only) ideas to take through market research and feasibility.

We promise you that the work ahead in market research and feasibility is not easy, so you can probably develop the business plan for only one social enterprise at a time unless your team is fairly large and can focus its efforts on more than one idea for social enterprise. After you've been through the entire process one time, you will be able to shorten the time involved in vetting succeeding social enterprise ideas.

The evaluation process is likely to involve a stimulating discussion as team members share their diverse perspectives and rankings.

One more point before you start ranking your great ideas. Occasionally, one member of the team may have strong opinions about an idea or the organization's leader has a preconceived idea about what the social enterprise should be. We have seen this happen more than once. That is one reason the ranking system, using objective criteria, can be such a valuable tool.

> One organization that developed a social enterprise program sings its praises: "We developed what we call our litmus test for decision making. Anything we consider we might do, we look at it and say, 'Is it in support of our mission and vision? Does it make sense for the individuals we serve? Does it make sense in terms of dollars and cents?' If it doesn't pass those three, we don't do it. We aren't going to do anything that is not profitable anymore."

stories from the real world

It may be that your team will agree to move forward with an idea for social enterprise that did not receive the highest numerical score. That's fine—as long as the entire team has endorsed the idea at this point.

Worksheet Twelve: Evaluate Your Earned Income Opportunities

Idea	Criterion 1	Criterion 2	Criterion 3	Criterion 4	Criterion 5	Criterion 6	Criterion 7	Criterion 8	Criterion 9	Score

Great work! You have narrowed your list of potential social enterprise ideas to one or two that you believe are the great idea(s). Now you must begin the rigorous work of proving that your great idea is, in fact, *great*.

To Recap

◆ Don't take your assets for granted. They might be rocket science to someone who doesn't do it every day.

◆ An objective decision-making process will prevent your team members from talking themselves into an idea just because they like it.

◆ Brainstorming will generate dozens of potential ideas for earned income, but the list must be narrowed to only the one or two with the highest potential for reaching your goals.

Chapter Six

Testing the Waters

IN THIS CHAPTER

···→ Introduction to market research

···→ Market push versus market pull

···→ Types of market research

···→ Your market research plan

···→ Benchmark time!

···→ Worksheets thirteen through twenty-three

Let's review what you have accomplished so far in this process of becoming a social entrepreneur. You have:

◆ developed and clarified your vision, mission, and core values;

◆ set mission and financial outcomes for earned income;

◆ developed an inventory of your assets;

◆ developed objective evaluation criteria;

◆ brainstormed earned income opportunities; and

◆ narrowed the list of good ideas to "The Great Idea(s)."

What Comes Next? Testing, Testing, and More Testing!

> You can't short-cut the time it takes to perform thorough market research and feasibility. This process will provide invaluable information to your organization both for the prospective social enterprise idea(s) and for your organization in general. Most teams spend several weeks on this part of the social enterprise process. It should test your assumptions and confirm that you are on the right track. You'll use all the valuable information you learn to profile customers and create an effective sales plan and business plan.
>
> **warning!**

Perhaps one of the most valuable lessons to be learned from this process is the importance of testing your assumptions. Sure, it looks like a great idea, but can you *prove* it? You cannot short-cut this part of the social enterprise process. Doing so will place your valuable organizational resources at risk. Testing takes time, but there is no substitute for testing all your assumptions to prove them … or modify them.

Chapters Six and **Seven** will give your team the tools you'll need to perform the market research and feasibility that will test your assumptions and confirm that you have chosen a viable earned income social enterprise opportunity.

Often at this stage in the process, many teams discover that what they thought was "The Great Idea" turns out not to be so great after all. This is not a failure. On the contrary, it could actually be considered a success. Why? Because your team did not rush into a social enterprise that could not reach your mission and dollar goals, or did not meet a demonstrated market need, or could place your valuable assets at risk.

The value of this social enterprise process lies in the benchmarks along the way that allow your team to reevaluate and modify your plans before you invest more into an earned income idea that isn't as feasible as you originally believed.

At this stage, if market research proves your great idea isn't so great after all, it might require you to go back to your asset inventory and select a different route to earned income. Don't be concerned if this is the case, and don't hold on to an idea that doesn't prove to be viable. Many teams have started over and found a better social enterprise in the process. And many teams have uncovered a completely different social enterprise idea as a result of getting out of the office and talking and listening to their potential clients/customers.

> A food bank just *knew* it had developed "The Great Idea" for social enterprise. It planned to use its commercial kitchen to produce specialty diet meals for small local day care and residential care businesses. But when the food bank tested the idea during market research, no one wanted this service. Going back to its asset inventory, the food bank discovered an underutilized physical asset. Its delivery trucks went out full every morning but returned empty (an underutilized physical asset). The food bank has begun to offer backhauling for a fee.
>
>  **stories from the real world**

Introduction to Market Research

Market research is the "systematic gathering, recording, and analyzing of data about challenges relating to the marketing of goods and services." When we speak about market research, we use a slightly different language from what you might be accustomed to hearing in the nonprofit world. For example, we say "customer" and "buyer" rather than "client" and "funder."

To be effective in the market, every organization must ask and answer these kinds of questions:

◆ Who are our potential buyers and end users? Are they the same or different? What are they like? Where are they located? Can they and will they buy and use what we are selling? What will motivate them to buy or use our enterprise?

◆ Are we offering the kinds of products, programs, or services customers want and need, at the best place, at the best time, and in the right quantities? What makes us unique?

◆ Are the features of our product, program, or service providing the benefits buyers and end users seek? How do we know?

◆ Will our prices be consistent with customers' perceptions of the value of our product, program, or service?

◆ What will make our promotional programs effective?

◆ What are our customers' perceptions of our business?

◆ How does our business compare with our competitors? Who are our competitors? What do we know about them? Can we compete effectively?

◆ How can we test and prove our assumptions?

Question: Would knowing the answers to these types of questions be useful in how you decide and deliver your current programs and services? If you performed regular market research about your current clients, funders, donors, volunteers, and others (customers), would you gain valuable information about how you are perceived in your community, how clients feel about the value of your programs and services, how donors and funders view your organization and more? We think so, and we encourage you to consider this as a valuable part of your organizational tool kit.

Why Do Market Research?

Effective and thorough market research is the key to identifying, selecting, and developing a successful social enterprise venture. Without thorough market research, you might choose a social enterprise idea that could turn out to be a learn-as-you-go (high probability of failure) program.

> Market research requires you to "Get Up and Get Out" (of the office) to test your assumptions. You've got to talk with potential customers to determine what they need, what they want, how much they will pay, how they want to take advantage of it, and more.
>
>

Think of market research as strategic risk management. Thorough market research will enable you to clearly see whether your social enterprise idea is feasible, both financially and organizationally.

Market Push Versus Market Pull

If you come up with a new program or service and then try to find a buyer for it, you are *pushing* your way into the marketplace. On the other hand, if you listen to your customers, clients, community, and even funders, hear what they say they want or need, and then deliver it, you are being *pulled* into the market.

This is a significant point to understand because it is usually easier and less risky to be *pulled* into a social enterprise than it is to *push* your way into a market that may not be interested in what you offer or is not willing to pay your price.

Here is some homework to complete right now. Turn whoever answers the phone at your organization into a data collector. Give that person a special notebook to record the questions they are asked when they answer the phone. In a few weeks, you will have collected important data that might lead you to a new social enterprise idea or change the way you promote yourself to clarify your programs and services or even have data that might have value to another organization (for a fee, of course).

> Turn the person who answers your phone into a data collector. Keep a record of all the questions your callers ask about your services, what you know, where you are located, and all the unrelated questions. Before you know it, you'll have collected valuable market data that just might turn into the idea for an avenue for earned income.
>
> **idea!**

Here's an example that occurred in an organization we worked with. The organization is a residential facility for families of childhood cancer patients. The receptionist kept a record of all calls and questions for several weeks. The social enterprise team reviewed the list and discovered that residents in their community had questions about kid-friendly programs, services, professionals, restaurants, and activities. The result? The organization is developing a directory of family-friendly opportunities, available for a fee.

Three Common Types of Market Research

There are three common types of market research that your team should consider in this social enterprise process:

◆ Your own backyard research

◆ Primary research

◆ Secondary research

Your Own Backyard Market Research

You may already know more than you realize. Ask questions about a proposed product, program, or service, and you are likely to discover that someone has knowledge and information that you need. Do not overlook the information in front of you.

Primary Research

Primary research can be as simple as asking potential customers how they feel about your potential social enterprise idea, as we just discussed. Or it can be as complex as surveys conducted by professional market research firms. Common types of primary research include the following:

◆ Direct-mail questionnaires

◆ Telephone surveys

◆ Focus groups

◆ Test marketing

◆ Experiments

◆ "Secret shopping" the competition or similar organizations

> Consider asking a college or university business school to help with market research. This could be a win-win collaboration. Students or interns need practical projects to complete their course work. Nonprofits with smaller staffs might find it difficult to complete thorough market research without help.
>
>  practical tip

Secondary Research

Secondary research takes advantage of existing published sources, such as surveys, books, and articles from professional or trade publications, that could help you formulate a new idea, test an assumption, or clarify your thinking by taking advantage of research that has already been done. Local sources of information tend to provide better research results because local markets may contradict regional or national trends. Trade associations and government agencies are rich sources of information. This type of research helps validate your primary research. Thankfully, much of this information is available over the Internet or even from local organizations at little or no cost.

Key Market Categories

There are three categories essential to gathering thorough market research data:

1. The overall market environment and market trends

2. Your buyer/target market

3. Your competition

The Overall Market Environment and Market Trends

The "market" is the environment of current and potential customers and buyers. You will want to research and understand trends in customer behaviors, demographic changes, growth of certain populations, product development, technology adaptation, buying and selling, and trends in market promotion.

The market is constantly evolving and challenging organizations to understand and adapt. It is not something that can be controlled. Only those with key technologies or those that are very large can realistically impact how the market behaves. Obviously, it is essential to understand as much as you can about the market to position your social enterprise to be a financial winner.

So, how do you gather this information?

Collecting Data

Begin market research by collecting your *assumptions* about market trends, your target market, and your competition. You can collect considerable data about market trends that affect not only your social enterprise idea but also your organization's market as a whole fairly easily by completing thorough Internet searches and creating a notebook of the research data.

Worksheets in this and the next chapter will focus on *testing* and *confirming* or *challenging* your assumptions. You cannot start a social enterprise without confirming that it's viable.

We suggest you review all the worksheets about market research in this chapter with your social enterprise team first and together identify the information you need. You can then divide the team accordingly and make specific assignments. A worksheet at the end of this chapter (worksheet twenty-three) can be used to outline your total research plan so you can manage the details.

We've deliberately placed the worksheet at the end of the chapter because you will need to identify all the pieces required by reviewing and discussing the worksheets first. Remember, these worksheets are guides to help you identify the critical aspects that go into a market research process. Use them as presented or modify them to meet your needs.

Schedule regular team meetings to share and compare your research results to confirm that your great idea is still *great*. If at any point in the research phase you question your great idea, now is the time to evaluate its viability, decide whether to continue or whether to go back, examine your asset inventory and list of potential ideas, and start over.

There is no shame in starting over! It is a sensible step to take in launching a *successful* social enterprise rather than pursuing something that simply won't work.

Typically, the market research phase of your social enterprise process takes at least six to eight weeks. You simply cannot short-cut this part of the process or rely on assumptions. Doing so will put your organization's valuable assets at risk.

You must find the answers to these questions and more:

1. What are the consumer trends in the market nationally, regionally, and locally for your proposed venture, product, program, or service? What do people buy, what motivates them to buy, etc.? You can find much of this on the Internet, but you will want to validate it specifically for your local area or proposed market area by asking questions of representatives of your target market itself.

2. Is the market for your proposed venture, product, program, or service growing or declining? Is it, or will it be, large enough to reach your mission and dollar goals? If the market isn't large enough to support your social enterprise, now is the time to step back and consider whether it is still viable.

3. Is technology changing potential buying opportunities or how customers learn about your proposed venture, product, program, or service? What effect will technology have on how you produce or deliver your social enterprise? How will it affect the way you produce or deliver your social enterprise to your target market?

4. What is the customer price sensitivity toward your proposed venture, product, program, or service? Is cost a critical factor, or will the customer pay more to get more? You can't afford to make assumptions here. You've got to talk to potential customers and clarify answers to the pricing question.

5. What will it cost to launch your venture, product, program, or service? What will it cost to stay competitive? This is one of the reasons that research about your competition is such a critical factor.

6. What promotional messages are you hearing and/or seeing regarding your proposed social enterprise or similar ones? Where are these messages? How often are they occurring? How effective are they? How will you measure their effectiveness? The answers to these questions will all become a valuable part of your sales plan.

> You simply cannot perform effective and thorough market research while sitting in your office. That will lead to assumptions that, if not tested and validated, could put your valuable assets at risk. Instead, you must "Get Up and Get Out," ask questions, get answers, and ensure that your social enterprise idea is feasible and will work!
>
> **warning!**

Worksheet Thirteen: Market Trends

First, list your assumptions on this worksheet. Then identify ways to test your assumptions, because you must test. You will find information about many of the broad market trends on the Internet. Other resources might include your university's department of economic research, community development corporations, chambers of commerce, and others whose business it is to track trends.

Market Trend	Impact of Trend at One to Three Years	Impact of Trend at Three to Five Years	How Can We Capitalize on the Trend?	Strategy to Minimize Risk Related to Trend
Example: population is aging	Increased demand for elder care is estimated at 45 percent increase.	Will continue to drain local resources of existing agencies.	Offer a package of elder services.	Continued research to validate needs.

As you delved into researching market trends, did you also uncover any valuable information that could affect how your organization will deliver its programs and services in the future? As you work through this social enterprise process, remember to consider how you can apply your market research findings into other organizational operations. That is one of the important added benefits to this complex process.

Shifting from Trends to Customers

Now it's time to begin the earnest work of identifying and profiling your potential customer(s). Some of the key things to learn in your research regarding your target market are:

◆ Who are your potential customers? What motivates them to buy? What do they say they want and need? Is your potential customer an individual, another nonprofit, or a for-profit business?

◆ Is the buyer the same as the end user? For example, the end user of a day care is the child in day care. The buyer is the parent or guardian. Each has different motivations, wants, and needs, so you'll need to divide up your research team to learn all you can if your buyers and end users are not the same.

◆ Where are your potential buyers and end users? How can you reach them? How will they take advantage of your social enterprise? Will you go to them? Will they come to you? Can you deliver over the Internet?

◆ How many potential customers are there? How big is the pool of potential customers? Is it growing, stable, or on the decline?

◆ What can you learn about the benefits customers expect from your social enterprise? Your focus has to be on the *benefits* customers say they want and need.

Market Research Part One: The Customer/Buyer/End User

Who will purchase or pay for your social enterprise because they benefit from what you offer? Who is the end user? Are they one and the same? It is important to know your target market as best you can because your resources are probably limited. Once you know the buyer and end user well, you can focus your efforts on the most effective ways to reach them to promote and deliver your social enterprise.

This isn't rocket science either. The easiest way to begin your market research and data collection is to talk to potential buyers and end users. Open a conversation by asking, "If we were to [name your product or service idea], would you be interested?" If the answer is yes, then ask more questions. Let the potential customer tell you what they want, what they'll pay, how they want to take advantage and more. Ask about price, ask about features, ask about promotion, ask about your competition, etc.

If the answers reflect little or no interest in your proposed social enterprise idea, ask why? Maybe you can modify your idea to better appeal to the target market. If your research at this point shows little or no interest, it is time to go back to the drawing board, review your asset inventory and other great ideas, and start over with a new idea.

Record the answers you receive in market research in the following worksheets.

If your buyer and end user are different, divide your team to focus on both, because everything you learn will be invaluable when you begin the work on sales planning and promotion. If the buyers and end users are different, the information learned is likely to be vastly different, so you

> Getting started on market research isn't hard. Start conversations with potential buyers or end users with "If we were to provide [business venture], would you be interested? If so, why? What benefits would you want to derive? What might you be willing to pay? Are you currently getting this product (or service)? What do you like about it? What would you change?"
>
>  practical tip

Consider the difference in motivation for buyer and end user in this example. You offer a vacation day care. The end user (child) is motivated by fun, toys, activities, food, friends, etc. The buyer (parent) is motivated by safety, nutrition, educational stimulation, etc. You simply cannot lump them together. This will become very clear when you develop your sales plan.

food for thought

might end up short-circuiting your sales success by lumping all this research into one category and making assumptions.

Complete worksheets fourteen through nineteen, and then take stock of where you are and what you have learned. Then identify your next steps. You may find that these worksheets do not meet your exact research needs. In that case, use them as a guide and create your own with additional (or different) details. The more research you do, the more likely your social enterprise will succeed!

Worksheet Fourteen: Buyer Profile

Start by collecting your team's assumptions here. Then analyze and validate them more carefully through market research. Complete a worksheet for each proposed social enterprise. Discard any unproved assumptions and list only your *validated* research information.

Proposed venture/product/program/service: _____

Buyer	Buying Decisions (Who makes the decision to buy? Is it the user or someone else? Describe.)	Demographic Description (age, income, occupation, ethnicity, level of education, family size, marital status, etc.)	Geographic Issues (Where do the buyers live? How can you best reach them?)	Other Important Characteristics of Buyer
Example: parent of preschool child.	Parent makes decisions, but child can be an influencer.	Mid- to upper-income single-parent family, primarily in trades or high tech.	Primarily in northern suburbs, very Internet savvy.	Status of child care is critical feature.

Worksheet Fifteen: End User Profile

Collect your assumptions here and then analyze and validate them more carefully through market research. Complete a worksheet for each proposed social enterprise. Discard any unproved assumptions and list only your *validated* research information.

	Demographics (age, income, occupation, ethnicity, level of education, family size, marital status, etc.)	Geographic Issues (Where do the users live? How can you best reach them?)	Other Important Characteristics of End User
Example: preschool child	Three- to five-year-old, single parent (female), various ethnicities, mostly boys.	Primarily in northern suburbs but involved in kid sport teams.	Wants sports-oriented day care activities.

Worksheet Sixteen: Size of the Buyer/User Market(s)

Collect your assumptions here and then analyze and validate them more carefully through market research. Complete a worksheet for each proposed social enterprise. Discard any unproved assumptions and list only your *validated* research information.

Proposed venture/product/program/service: _____

Buyer(s)	Size of Market Today	Growth Potential Three to Five Years Out	Growth Curve (slow, moderate, rapid)
Example: parent of preschool child	Northern suburbs have 78 percent of families with preschool children.	Projected to remain at 75 percent with new families entering area.	Flat.

End User	Size of Market Today	Growth Potential Three to Five Years Out	Growth Curve (slow, moderate, rapid)
Example: preschool child	See above.	See above, but uncertain whether will remain boy centered.	Flat, but male/female mix may vary.

Features and Benefits

This next exercise will likely challenge the traditional nonprofit way of thinking. Historically, most nonprofits have produced brochures and websites extolling all the wonderful things they do—their history, their accomplishments, their facilities, and so on. These promotional pieces become a laundry list of *features.*

On the other hand, what motivates customers to pay for and use your social enterprise or buy your products, programs, and services are the *benefits* they receive.

Benefits are defined by your customer. *Features* describe *how* you deliver the benefits to your customer.

Worksheet Seventeen: Practice—Features and Benefits

Let's try this out. Discuss this with your team and list all the *features* and *benefits* you can think of for some everyday items. Remember that benefits are defined by the customer and features define how you will deliver the benefits.

Item	Features	Benefits
Product: microwave popcorn	Example: comes in a disposable bag	Example: easy cleanup—no pan to wash
Service: bilingual counseling	Example: provides Spanish and Chinese sessions	Example: understands your culture, speaks your language
Program: homeless shelter	Example: open twenty-four hours	Example: access in all types of weather
Venture: coffee shop run by clients	Example: training for ex-felons	Example: job-readiness certificate for graduates

As you develop your promotional strategies and materials in **Chapter Seven**, it is critical that you understand and promote the *benefits* of your social enterprise. You won't have to guess about this, because you will have confirmed the features and benefits of your social enterprise that your customers say they want through prior thorough market research.

Additional Homework

Review your current agency brochures, website, or other promotional materials. Are they focused on features or benefits?

practical tip

Worksheet Eighteen: Features and Benefits

Complete a worksheet for each of your proposed ventures. Confirm your assumptions and validate them through market research. Discard any unproved assumptions and list only your *validated* research information.

Proposed venture/product/program/service: _____

Benefits Defined by the Buyer/End User	Features Needed to Deliver Benefits
◆ _____	◆ _____
◆ _____	◆ _____
◆ _____	◆ _____
◆ _____	◆ _____
◆ _____	◆ _____
◆ _____	◆ _____
◆ _____	◆ _____
◆ _____	◆ _____
◆ _____	◆ _____

Buyer and End User Priorities

What is important to your potential customer? The only way to find this out is to include this question in your market research. Does the customer or end user make decisions based on service? Quality? Location? Variety? Price? Convenience? Uniqueness? You can't assume these answers. These will be critical parts of your sales plan in **Chapter Seven**.

Worksheet Nineteen: Buyer and End User Priorities

Complete a worksheet for each of your proposed ventures. List what you have learned on the worksheet with the highest priority first. Confirm and validate your assumptions through market research. Discard any unproved assumptions and list only your *validated* research information.

Buyer Priority	Importance	Why?

End User Priority	Importance	Why?

Results of Customer Market Research

Let's take a break here to take stock of where you are, what you have learned, and what is still left to learn about your target market. Use this next worksheet to gather your research results. This is the time to confirm that "The Great Idea" is still the *right idea*. Again, there is no shame in abandoning the original great idea if you are uncertain, if you've discovered evidence that it won't meet your objective criteria or your original mission and dollar goals. If you have divided the research among team members, ask them to gather and share their research notes so that you have a complete picture of your research to date.

Worksheet Twenty: Results of Customer Market Research

Market research is hard. It takes time and energy. However, it is well worth the energy you put into it. Absolutely nothing takes the place of learning beforehand all you can about the viability of your social enterprise so that you don't put your organization's valuable resources at risk. Frankly, many organizations get bogged down at this point, rush into the enterprise too soon, or abandon the process entirely. We strongly recommend that you consider engaging a consultant or market researcher to help you navigate this process and keep you focused and on target.

important

What were the most valuable things you learned about your potential buyer(s)?	◆ _____ ◆ _____ ◆ _____
What were the most valuable things you learned about the end user(s)?	◆ _____ ◆ _____ ◆ _____

Based on what you have learned about your buyer/end user market, can you achieve your mission and financial outcomes as stated when you began this process?	
What were the most valuable research tools?	◆ _____ ◆ _____ ◆ _____
What were the stumbling blocks, and how did you overcome them?	
Is this venture, product, program, or service still the right one?	
If so, why? If not, why not?	

Unanswered Questions and Next Steps

It is unlikely that your customer market research is finished. In fact, market research should become a regular part of your management plan from this point forward. Ensure that you never make decisions based on assumptions, especially those made in a vacuum (without outsider input). Test, test, test, and constantly challenge your assumptions.

Because this is so important, take a few minutes, right now, to plan the next steps in your customer market research.

Worksheet Twenty-One: Next Steps in Customer Market Research

Buyer(s)	What We Haven't Tested	Test/Research Method(s)	Responsibility	Target Date

End User(s)	What We Haven't Tested	Test/Research Method(s)	Responsibility	Target Date

Market Research Part Two: The Competition

A critical part of your market research is understanding your competition. As you interview and research your potential customers, include questions about your current or potential competition.

Your competition is any business or organization that will compete directly or indirectly with your social enterprise. It is essential to understand your competition and be clear about who or what it is. This might not be as obvious as you think at first glance.

Here is why you must understand your competition:

◆ To define your unique competitive advantage (if there is one). This is what makes you different from/better than your competition. Promoting your competitive advantage will be a critical part of your sales plan.

◆ To determine whether there is room for your social enterprise in the marketplace. If you can't compete successfully, maybe you shouldn't launch this social enterprise after all. This is another critical benchmark in the process.

> Market research about your competition is the "secret shopping" part of this process. Call, visit, buy, ask customers, read reviews. Learn everything you can about your competition.
>
> **!** important

Direct Competition

Direct competition is a nonprofit or for-profit business that offers the same product, service, or program as your social enterprise. Direct competition does not have to be local. For example, can a customer get the product or service online?

Here is an example: A nonprofit sells jewelry created by its disabled clients. Imagine how large its competitive market is. The nonprofit will need to define the local competition, Internet competition, and specialty competition, and it will need to define clearly its competitive advantage over each competitor.

Another example: A nonprofit community theater found that while it had only four obvious direct competitors (other amateur companies) in its community, it had several other competitors, such as movie theaters, home movie rentals, and sports and other entertainment venues. What could make the nonprofit different from/better than its competition?

Indirect Competition

An indirect competitor offers something different that competes for your target market's money. By understanding your competition, you can better understand what obstacles you face and how best to succeed in a crowded marketplace. This information will be critical as you define your sales strategies in **Chapter Seven**.

Worksheet Twenty-Two: Direct and Indirect Competition

Collect your assumptions here and then analyze and validate them more carefully through market research. Complete a worksheet for each proposed venture, product, program, or service. Discard any unproved assumptions and list only your *validated* research information.

Proposed venture/product/program/service: _____

Competition	Direct or Indirect?	Strengths (What makes them good?)	Weaknesses (Where are they vulnerable?)	How can we compete? (What is our competitive advantage?)

Develop Your Market Research Plan

The worksheets in this chapter have outlined many of the questions you must answer about market trends, market size, customer needs, your competition, and more. Now use the next worksheet to outline your plan to test your initial assumptions and to add all the additional information you will gather when you talk to potential customers, buyers, and end users. Again, use these worksheets to get started and develop additional worksheets as needed to perform thorough and rigorous market research.

Worksheet Twenty-Three: Outline Your Customer Market Research Plan

Buyer(s)	What We Need to Know	Research Methods to Be Used	Team Member(s) Responsible	Target Dates
End User(s)	**What We Need to Know**	**Research Methods to Be Used**	**Team Member(s) Responsible**	**Target Dates**

Benchmark Time

It's now time to take stock of where you are before you move to the next step in the social enterprise process. Are you on track?

> *Did it work the way we thought it would? No. But would we be a $4.3 million agency in year four from inception [of the social enterprise]? No, absolutely not. Again, as hokey as that sounds, we would never be where we are today without [the social enterprise training].*
>
> Clara R.

Go back to **Chapter Four** and review your vision, mission, core values, and goals. Now is the time to make an informed decision about whether to continue with this social enterprise idea or go back to your asset inventory and select a more likely idea to be taken through market research and feasibility.

Don't talk yourself into an idea if your research has proved that your great idea is not as great as you thought. If you need to return to your asset inventory and do some additional brainstorming, we promise that you will find the market research phase easier the second time.

To Recap

◆ Whew! Thorough market research takes time, but you cannot take shortcuts.

◆ You have to learn all you can about buyers and end users to validate your social enterprise idea before you go farther.

◆ Can you compete? It is critical to define your competitive advantage.

◆ Reality check: Is your social enterprise idea still valid?

Chapter Seven

Developing Your Sales Plan

IN THIS CHAPTER

- ⋯→ Elements in a sales plan

- ⋯→ Market position

- ⋯→ Pricing strategies

- ⋯→ Distribution methods

- ⋯→ Promotional strategies

- ⋯→ Testing your assumptions

- ⋯→ Worksheets twenty-four through twenty-nine

Question: What is the difference between creating a sales plan for a for-profit business and creating one for your nonprofit business?

Answer: Essentially, a sales plan is a sales plan. The real difference, and it can mean a significant edge, is your nonprofit's mission. While it would be foolish to assume that people will flock to your social enterprise simply because you are a nonprofit with a mission, it is safe to assume that there are some current and potential customers who will choose to buy from you rather than a for-profit business simply because you have a mission, *all other things being equal* (or nearly equal).

The trick is to put these assumptions aside for now and build a comprehensive and *strategic* sales plan that will help you meet your social enterprise goals. This might be another

> You cannot assume that customers will pay for your social enterprise just because you are a nonprofit. Your nonprofit status can be considered a competitive advantage only if *the product or service you offer is as good as or better than what is offered by a for-profit competitor.*
>
> **warning!**

opportunity to collaborate with a business school, university, or college in your area. Students need projects to complete their course work, and you could benefit greatly from their expertise.

Let's review: Your market research helped you understand your customers, what motivates them to buy, and the features they desire. You also examined your competition and defined your competitive edge.

Refresher Exercise: Features and Benefits

Referring back to your market research, list two or three benefits customers will enjoy with your social enterprise. Then identify two or three features required to deliver the benefits.

Remember: Benefits are defined by the customer. Features describe the venture, program, or service you offer and how you will deliver the venture, program, or service.

Our social enterprise is _____

Benefits to the Customer	Features to Deliver the Benefits

At this stage in the process, you are beyond making assumptions. Your market research about customers and competition has clearly defined what your customers want and need and how you can compete effectively. Now it is time to bring all that research forward to develop your sales plan. After all, if no one knows about your social enterprise, they can't take advantage of it and all your work is wasted. Your sales plan will include all the elements required to promote your social enterprise and make it available to your target market.

Steps to Create Your Sales Plan

1. Focus on the market(s) with the highest potential.

2. Establish your position in the marketplace.

3. Identify distribution methods.

4. Set a pricing strategy.

5. Develop promotional strategies.

> Your sales plan identifies a target market, then establishes your market position, the price of the social enterprise, distribution, and promotion. It defines how you will deliver what your customers said they want and need.
>
> practical tip

Focus on High-Potential Target Market(s)

Rather than wasting valuable resources on trying to reach every possible potential market, you will need to identify the markets that will have the highest return on your investment and help you reach your previously stated mission and dollar goals. You should have developed a list of potential customers in your research phase.

Worksheet Twenty-Four: Target Market

List potential customers with the highest buying potential. This is your target market.

Buyer(s)	End User(s)

Establish Your Position in the Marketplace

Now go back and review the market research on your highest potential customers. What did they say will motivate them to buy? What are the benefits they desire?

You will need to establish a position for each target market (buyer/end user) that will position you favorably.

Examples of Market Positioning

◆ High end. Your venture, program, product, or service is unique, has little competition, and is the "Jaguar" selection. You may not need to sell many to reach your goals.

◆ Low cost, low budget. Your venture, program, product, or service is priced very competitively. You will require a high volume of sales to reach your goals.

◆ Superior service or experience. Often, customers are not influenced by price but by the superior service or experience they receive. Consider a day at the spa or golf at a four-star resort versus buying beauty products at a big box store or playing putt-putt.

Worksheet Twenty-Five: Market Position

In your market research, you learned how to position your social enterprise in the market. Your customers told you which of the options above would work best.

State your market position on this worksheet.

Target Market	Market Position	Why?
Example: single female head of household (buyer)	Buyer wants combo of low cost and superior service.	Buyer is frugal but requires exceptional experience for child.
Example: preschool child (user)	User wants superior experience.	User wants to have fun.

Identify Distribution Methods

How will customers and end users access your social enterprise? Will they come to you? Will you deliver to them directly or through another venue? How will the product or service be packaged? How will these distribution methods affect your costs? Remember to refer to your earlier market research with potential customers who told you how they want to access your social enterprise.

Examples of Distribution Methods

◆ Customers can access your enterprise via the Internet.

◆ Customers will come to your site.

◆ Customers can purchase printed materials (books, workbooks, disks, etc.).

◆ You will need to deliver the product to customers.

Worksheet Twenty-Six: Distribution Methods

What did your customers tell you about how they would take advantage of your social enterprise?

Target Market(s)	Distribution Method(s)	Distribution Costs

Set Your Pricing Strategy

Again, go back and review your market research and what you learned about your target market(s). Review your market position. Estimate the true costs of delivering your enterprise venture. We'll clarify all costs in the next chapter. Based on what you know, you can now set a pricing strategy. It may have to be modified after you delve more deeply into the costs to start up and run your social enterprise, but it's okay to make an assumption at this point. This is another critical benchmark in the process.

Examples of Pricing Strategies

◆ *Competition based.* What does the competition charge for the same or similar product or service? Can you beat the competition on price, still achieve your goals, and meet customer demands?

◆ *Demand based.* If the demand for your enterprise venture is high, you might be able to lower the price and achieve your goals through volume sales. If the demand is low, you may have to look more carefully at buyer habits to see if you can justify the venture in the long run.

◆ *Value based.* If your market position is superior service or experience, you may find that you can charge a higher price for your enterprise venture. Remember, value is set by what the *customer perceives*, not what you perceive.

◆ *Cost-plus based.* This may be the most common pricing strategy and the one you will want to explore first. You merely take the costs of providing your enterprise venture and add the profit (markup) required to reach your goals.

Many organizations set their pricing strategy as a blend of one or more of these options, but keep in mind the results of your market research and resist the "charity-think" mode of underpricing your valuable social enterprise. Your goal is to make money!

Worksheet Twenty-Seven: Pricing Strategy

Define your pricing strategy based on market research into your customers and competition.

Pricing Strategy for Target Market: Buyer Market
Why?

Pricing Strategy for Target Market: End User
Why?

Develop Promotional Strategies

How will customers learn about your social enterprise? How will you reach them? What method(s) will be the most cost effective? Review your market research about what motivates your customer(s) to buy, where they are located, what benefits they want, and how you will compete.

Examples of Promotional Strategies

◆ *Personal selling.* Will you need to hire or contract with someone to sell your social enterprise? You can't just post something on your website and wait for the sales to roll in.

◆ *Incentive programs, e.g., frequent-use cards.* Do you need to provide incentives so that your customers will repeat their buying?

◆ *Bulk discounts.* Can the customer buy more or use more and pay less? Will you benefit from this strategy as well?

◆ *Advertising (media, print, Internet, etc.).* How will you tell potential customers about your social enterprise? Will you use Internet email blasts, newsletters, etc.? Send promotional materials via the US Mail? Set up booths at professional association meetings, conferences, and trade shows? There are costs involved in all promotional methods, so choose the most effective. (Your customers told you the answer.)

◆ *Co-branding, co-advertising.* Is there the potential for collaboration with another provider or advertiser?

◆ *Direct mail or other promotion.* Will you need a plan to repeat the advertising message throughout the year?

Worksheet Twenty-Eight: Promotional Strategy(s)

Identify your promotional strategy(s) for each target market.

Promotional Strategy for Target Market: Buyer
Why?

Promotional Strategy for Target Market: End User
Why?

Test Your Sales Strategies

Now is the time to "Get Up and Get Out" again to test your assumptions and strategies one more time.

Select representatives of your target market(s) and test your sales strategies for effectiveness. This exercise will not only affirm your strategies, but it can also be the first step in real sales as your target market(s) learn more about your social enterprise.

Use the next worksheet to put what you have learned about your social enterprise into a concise format. Then present your strategy to your target market representatives and record their responses. You can then make adjustments as needed to meet your customers' needs.

Think of the different approaches taken by the sellers of Jaguars versus the sellers of two-ton pickup trucks. The well-dressed Jaguar buyers see themselves driving up to a beautiful building in a sleek, shiny car with subtle music playing in the background. The rugged drivers of pickup trucks see themselves driving up in a cloud of dust, with a heavy load in the back, and thumping music.

Why are they different? The sellers' advertising responded to customer research and gave their very different customers what they said they would respond to.

 practical tip

Worksheet Twenty-Nine: Test Your Assumptions

Social enterprise: _____

Target market/buyer(s): _____

Target market/end user(s): _____

Benefits to buyer/user (what they told you they wanted):

◆ _____

◆ _____

◆ _____

◆ _____

◆ _____

Their buying priorities (what they told you mattered):

◆ _____

◆ _____

◆ _____

◆ _____

◆ _____

Market position: _____

Pricing strategy: _____

Distribution methods (how they said they want to take advantage of your social enterprise):

◆ _____

◆ _____

◆ _____

Promotional strategies:

◆ _____

◆ _____

◆ _____

Feedback received: _____

What appeared to work? _____

What needs to be modified or changed? _____

Other notes: _____

_____

_____

_____

_____

To Recap

◆ A sales plan is a vital element in your social enterprise strategies.

◆ Your sales plan should include important data learned in your market research phase.

◆ A sales plan includes positioning, pricing, distribution, and promotion.

Chapter Eight

Understanding Pricing, Financing, and Costs

IN THIS CHAPTER

- ···➤ Defining costs
- ···➤ Case study
- ···➤ Identifying your social enterprise costs
- ···➤ Financing options
- ···➤ Unrelated business income tax
- ···➤ Worksheet thirty

Y ou are now well on your way to the launch of your social enterprise. You have completed the market research that tested your assumptions about your customers and your competition. You have either confirmed that you have selected the great idea for earned income or retraced your steps and selected a different idea and carefully researched it to determine its feasibility. You have developed a sales plan.

The last major hurdle to overcome in this process is to identify and understand all the costs involved in establishing and maintaining your proposed social enterprise. This is another opportunity to collaborate with a business school, college, or university to gain valuable assistance in identifying all the costs required to launch and maintain your social enterprise.

Cost Analysis and Break-Even Point

One of the most overlooked aspects in evaluating the viability and sustainability of an earned income venture (not to mention *all* your current operations, programs, and services) is calculating the real and total costs to operate and maintain it. Without knowing the true costs, you will either underprice your social enterprise and lose money or overprice it and run the risk of being too expensive for your target market. Additionally, you will need to set up a separate account system for your social enterprise, rather than lumping it in with other expenses. How else can you calculate real expenses, and determine profit?

There are three steps to your costing analysis:

1. Identify all categories of costs. This is *not* done the same way you record costs for a grant or a fundraising program. You need to identify all the categories of costs of running a social enterprise business venture.

> Many organizations that have planned social enterprises have used the same detailed costing analysis to evaluate their current programs, services, and even traditional funding sources. Often, discovering the true costs involved in researching, writing, producing, and reporting a grant might show it is not as feasible as it once looked. The same can be said in understanding the true costs involved in a fundraising program or special event.
>
> **observation**

2. Allocate costs appropriately. We are talking here about details to the level of counting the ceiling tiles in the area to be used, the percentage of staff time and resources, the percentage of organizational resources required, the cost of contracting outside labor, etc.

3. Calculate the total costs and determine the break-even point. This is another important benchmark in your social enterprise process. Review your mission and dollar goals and your objective criteria. Does this great idea still work? If you need to break even and realize a net profit in eight months and your costing analysis shows that isn't feasible, something has to change.

Important Definitions

Now we will embark on a whole new type of costing. You are probably very adept at costing for grants, for special events, maybe even for your services. Your new business-think will require a different set of costing definitions, such as:

◆ *Fixed costs.* Those costs that remain constant regardless of changes in the level of activity. Examples include overhead, equipment, taxes, insurance, management salaries, rent, depreciation, advertising, etc.

◆ *Variable costs.* Those costs that change in proportion to changes in volume or that are directly related to the social enterprise itself. Materials and hourly labor are generally variable. When orders go up or down, so do these costs. Other examples of variable costs could include clerical costs, shipping, office supplies, travel, etc.

◆ *Direct costs.* Those costs that are associated directly with the development, production, or delivery of your social enterprise. These costs can be either fixed or variable.

◆ *Indirect costs.* Those costs that must be allocated or assigned to a particular product or service. They are incurred as a consequence of general overall operating activities often called overhead, i.e., rent, utilities. These costs can be either fixed or variable.

> **Total cost:** The total cost is equal to the variable costs plus the fixed costs. TC (total costs) = VC (variable costs) + FC (fixed costs), or to put it another way, TC (total costs) = indirect costs + direct costs.

◆ *Break-even point.* The point where revenue generated (fees, sales, etc.) equals total costs incurred. At the break-even point, profits will be zero. You've got to identify when the break-even point will happen in your business planning so that you can begin to generate a profit to reach the mission and dollar goals you set way back in the beginning of this process.

Case Study: KidPrep Agency

This case study of a representative (but fictional) nonprofit will illustrate the detailed cost analysis you must complete for your social enterprise. Let's pretend that your team has been hired to help calculate the costs and break-even point for this organization's proposed social enterprise.

KidPrep is a nonprofit that offers educational and recreational programs for children ages three to eighteen. Originally created to provide services to low-socioeconomic families, KidPrep has expanded to fill a niche in the market for two-wage-earner families.

KidPrep has a multiroom facility located on six acres of land that has mature landscaping, a ropes course, and three horses with a stable. Facilities include a gymnasium, kitchen, dining hall, and large conference hall with a contemporary sound system. The facility also has eight cabins that sleep up to four adults each. The cabins are rustic, with guests sharing bathhouses.

KidPrep is proposing a social enterprise to counter rising costs of its operations since money granted by the state is in jeopardy. Money from foundations and individual donations has been harder to procure the past five years.

One of KidPrep's social enterprise ideas is to rent its facilities to local companies and nonprofits for conferences and retreats. After doing thorough market research to validate that there is a demand for this service, KidPrep must now calculate costs to see whether they can offer a price that is both competitive and profitable.

The total cost of the venture and the break-even point is currently unknown. Listed below are many of the costs KidPrep has provided:

Fixed Costs	Notes	Cost per Year
Salary	Will require 25 percent of a salaried employee's time at an annual salary of $36,000 and benefits of $1,475.	
Sales and promotions	Sales presentations, meetings, and luncheons: $2,100 for the first year. Direct mail: $425 for the first year. Professional sales materials: ◆ Graphic designer: $3,000 ◆ Printed materials: $2,500	
Rent/mortgage	$3,800/month. Percentage of office space of the employee who will head up the project is calculated at 4.75 percent of total square footage.	
Transportation	Estimated at thirty miles/week, calculated at fifty-five cents/mile.	
Utilities	$10,300 per year. Estimated at 5 percent of total.	
Equipment purchases	Laptop computer with wireless Internet access: $1,200. Color printer: $175. Four ink cartridges: $25 each. Eight reams paper: $30 each. Projector: $350.	
Accounting	In-house. Estimated at 10 percent of employee's time. Annual salary of $46,500 and $1,450 in benefits.	
	Total Fixed Costs	$
	Variable Costs	
Housekeeping	Daily housekeeping during a two-day stay is thirty minutes per cabin for two people. Cost to clean is $25. Housekeeping after retreat is estimated at one hour at $25.	
Food	Outsourced to caterers. Estimated at $150/person total for two days.	
Other costs	Local tax:_____ Insurance:_____ Other:_____	
	Total Variable Costs	$

Calculate Breakeven for KidPrep

Assume KidPrep will sell a two-day retreat at $125 per person. Breakeven is the point at which revenue generated (fees, sales, etc.) equals total costs incurred. At the break-even point, profit will be zero.

Calculate either the number of attendees or number of retreats needed per year to reach breakeven.

Break-even point for KidPrep is reached at _____ attendees or _____ retreats per year.

Identify Costs for Your Social Enterprise

Now it is time to sharpen your pencil and identify all the potential costs that will be incurred for your social enterprise. The KidPrep exercise showed you how to think about costs. For this exercise, identify whether the cost is *per year*, *per month*, or *per unit*. Then allocate the cost appropriately.

Refer to your market research and sales plans for anticipated costs. Use this worksheet as an example or create your own, but be sure to anticipate and include *all costs*.

Worksheet Thirty: Your Anticipated Social Enterprise Costs

Cost	Per Year/ Per Month/ Per Unit	Fixed	Variable	Direct	Indirect
Labor (salaries plus benefits)					
Sales/promotions: ◆ _____ ◆ _____ ◆ _____ ◆ _____ ◆ _____					
Distribution: ◆ _____ ◆ _____ ◆ _____ ◆ _____ ◆ _____					
Rent/mortgage (percentage to venture)					
Transportation					
Utilities (percentage to venture)					
Equipment: ◆ _____ ◆ _____ ◆ _____ ◆ _____					

Cost	Per Year/ Per Month/ Per Unit	Fixed	Variable	Direct	Indirect
Taxes: ◆ Employee ◆ Sales					
Accounting					
Other: ◆ _____ ◆ _____ ◆ _____ ◆ _____ ◆ _____ ◆ _____					
Total costs					

Break-Even Point

Breakeven is critical to determine, because if you don't make enough sales to equal the costs, your organization will lose money on your social enterprise.

You will need to establish how often to evaluate sales to determine if you are losing money, making money, or breaking even. While this is usually done on an annual basis, in the early stages, you may wish to evaluate it on a quarterly or monthly basis to keep a close eye on expenses and revenue.

It is important that you set up a separate accounting system for your social enterprise to track costs and income, calculate taxes due (if any), and truly determine its feasibility.

important

Keep in mind that many businesses and organizations do not hit the break-even point until their second or third year, as the costs to start a venture could consume more resources in the first year or two. This is especially true in the case of launching a new product, program, or service. If your social enterprise involves modifying something you are currently doing, the time from start-up to profit is likely to be considerably shorter.

Calculate Your Break-Even Point

How many _____ are required per _____ to reach your break-even point? Realistically, how long will it take to reach breakeven? Refer to your objective criteria and initial dollar goals as a final benchmark to confirm that your great idea is still great.

Contributions versus Financing

Okay, now comes a really hard part. You are probably not used to dealing with money in any way except asking others to contribute through donations, grants, special events, and other traditional fundraising sources. Let us challenge you to change that mindset. You are a business with a nonprofit tax status, not a money-losing organization.

> If you are not on target with breakeven and potential profit, this is another opportunity to make adjustments, abandon the great idea for another idea, or make an informed decision to continue the social enterprise process.
>
> **observation**

The next few paragraphs will offer food for thought about potential sources of seed money, should you need it to underwrite the start-up costs of your social enterprise, and they will explore the difference between contributions and financing.

Contributions

Whether it is an individual charitable contribution or a grant, the donor has no expectation of financial return. You could call this free money in that it costs you nothing to use it—but is it really free? No, it often has strings attached, and there is always a cost to raising money.

Nationally, unrestricted giving has been on a downward trend for the past several years. Restricted giving is up because donors have become more sophisticated and at the same time more demanding as to how their contributions are spent. This is great for popular programs but makes it tough to start new programs or meet unpopular needs. For example, it's easier to raise money for kids but often harder to raise money for seniors.

> Many sources of traditional fundraising have strings attached and can be considered restricted revenue. Social enterprise generates unrestricted revenue that is yours to spend on priorities identified by your organization's leaders.
>
> **food for thought**

Historically, nonprofits take contributions, spend the money on the mission you agreed to spend it on, report back to the donor if required, and go looking for more money to repeat the process for next year. Not a bad solution, and we've all been doing it for years, but donor expectations have changed.

Financing Options

Major donors are now looking more and more for ways to *invest* in your mission, with the expectation of a return—not only for themselves but for you as well. They want to see sustainability in your organization so you can continue the mission both you and they feel is important.

So where do you get the money before you have created an earned income stream or, in many cases, to get the earned income stream flowing? This often requires an initial financial investment that you might not have available. It also usually requires that you pay it back.

And, a critical component in requesting financial investment of any kind is your business plan.

Here are some of the ways that financing works:

Loan

A loan can be either a personal loan from an individual or a loan from a traditional lending institution.

- ◆ Lenders usually review either your cash flow or unencumbered underperforming assets.

- ◆ Past financial performance of your nonprofit is very important to lenders.

- ◆ The character of senior officers and board members is a strong concern for the lender.

- ◆ The lender has the expectation of financial return.

- ◆ The nonprofit must begin to pay back the loan immediately, usually on a monthly basis.

Recoverable Grant

A grant is made in the traditional manner. The grantor gives a nonprofit funds to initiate, support, or sustain a particular program, service, or social enterprise.

- ◆ The grantor requires the nonprofit and grantor to agree on financial performance goals prior to funding.

- ◆ If goals are met, the grant converts to a loan and is paid back.

- ◆ If goals are not met, the grant reverts to normal no-repayment grant status.

Nonprofit Lending

A nonprofit lending program is a specialized program offered by limited-lending institutions. These might include banks, consortiums of "angel" investors, or others whose investments and loans are designed specifically for nonprofits.

- ◆ The rate is competitive or below market rate.

- ◆ The loan must be paid back.

Bond

A bond is a debt you sell to private individuals.

◆ Interest is paid semiannually.

◆ Principal is paid back at maturity as specified in the bonding agreement.

Unrelated Business Income Tax Defined

A potential consequence for nonprofits and social enterprise is unrelated business income tax (UBIT), which we mentioned earlier. Rather than being afraid of this consequence, we advise you to get professional advice about whether your social enterprise will likely result in a taxable event. If so, build it into the cost of doing business and pay the tax. In any case, you don't have to worry about UBIT until you have made a profit. It's that simple.

> It is important to plan for and understand the potential that revenue generated by your social enterprise revenue could be considered unrelated business income and be taxable. Don't stress about this. Get professional advice from a legal or tax professional with nonprofit expertise, plan for it when you cost your enterprise, and pay the tax.

important

According to the IRS currently, an activity such as a social enterprise is an unrelated business (and subject to business income tax) if it meets all three of the following standards:

1. It is a trade or business.

2. It is regularly carried on.

3. It is not substantially related to furthering the exempt purpose of the organization.

There are several exemptions to the issue of UBIT, including resale of donated goods, such as in a thrift store, or if the social enterprise is run primarily by volunteers. You will want to investigate this thoroughly in your social enterprise costing and planning.

What's most important here is that you identify any potential tax implications of your social enterprise, including UBIT or even sales tax. We strongly suggest that you contact an accounting or legal professional with nonprofit expertise to gain the benefit of their qualified advice.

Plan ahead. If it is likely that your enterprise revenue will be taxable, build it into the cost of doing business and pay the tax. You certainly don't want to get a surprise visit from the IRS at a later date with a statement of tax due plus penalties and interest!

Disclaimer

The above definition of unrelated business income tax is intended to provide a general definition. There are, however, a number of modifications, exclusions, and exceptions to the general definition of unrelated business income. Please refer to IRS Publication 598 (Tax on

Unrelated Business Income of Exempt Organizations) for current rules and regulations. Also confer with your own tax consultant. We cannot provide tax advice, counsel, or consultation and, as such, expressly take no responsibility for any tax liability for any venture created as a result of utilizing information in this manual.

To Recap

◆ It is critical that you identify and allocate all costs of doing business as they relate to your social enterprise.

◆ After the break-even point, profit can begin to accrue.

◆ Unrelated business income may be subject to tax. If so, build it into the cost of doing business and pay it.

◆ Financing options may be available for your social enterprise for start-up costs.

Chapter Nine

Developing Your Business Plan

IN THIS CHAPTER

···→ Business plan format

···→ Looking back—what have you learned?

···→ Goals and next steps

···→ Worksheet thirty-one

Congratulations! We hope that by now you have followed all the steps in this manual, performed thorough market research and feasibility studies, and are ready to turn your great idea into a social enterprise.

The final step in the social enterprise process is to develop a business plan. As we previously emphasized, the business plan will keep you on track and provide benchmarks for achievement. It presents a format that gathers all your valuable research and plans into a concise format. It can be a valuable presentation tool for stakeholders, and it can springboard the discussion with funders and financers if seed money is required.

We offer the following simplified business plan template as the final step in your social enterprise process. This format makes it easy to gather your data into one place. Use this format, create your own, or search the Internet for other versions. Regardless of what format you use, we assure you that omitting this vital step in the process could negate all your valuable work so far.

> *We believe in this process. It was like a sermon. It gave us a new way of thinking: How can we sustain our program? In social service, there is the old way of doing things: We depend on the grant; we depend on state and federal funds. Now it is okay, you can self-sustain, you can depend on you.*
>
> Harriet S.

If you've followed the steps outlined in this manual, creating the business plan will not be difficult. Remember that at this phase in the process, there can be no assumptions. You have asked all the right questions and gotten the answers you need to launch a successful social enterprise—or you have elected to refine your current programs and services to become more efficient and effective. If the latter is your choice, we'll bet that you have found some new revenue streams as a result.

Congratulations!

The Basic Business Plan

The business plan for _____ (name of social enterprise)

Presented by _____ for _____ (organization)

Describe the social enterprise.

How this social enterprise supports organization's mission:

_____

_____

_____

_____

Mission goals for this social enterprise:

◆ _____

◆ _____

◆ _____

Money goals for this social enterprise:

◆ _____

◆ _____

◆ _____

Target customers (answer for each target customer):

	Who Are They? Where Are They?	Size of the Target Market	Growth Potential of Target Market
Group one			
Group two			
Group three			

Customer needs that will be addressed by this social enterprise include:

_____

_____

_____

_____

How did you prove these assumptions?

◆ _____

◆ _____

◆ _____

◆ _____

Is the buyer different from the end user (describe both)?

_____

_____

_____

_____

Buyer/end user's primary priorities that influence them to purchase and use this social enterprise:

◆ _____

◆ _____

◆ _____

◆ _____

Primary competition. Their strengths and weaknesses:

Competitor	Product, Pricing	Strengths	Weaknesses

Our competitive advantage:

_____

_____

_____

_____

Our promotional strategies:

◆ To stakeholders

◆ To buyers

◆ To end users

Our pricing strategy:

_____

_____

_____

_____

Our distribution methods:

_____

_____

_____

_____

Start-up costs:

Item	Amount	Potential Revenue Source

Ongoing costs:

Item	Amount	Potential Revenue Source

Annual financial projections:

	First Quarter	Second Quarter	Third Quarter	Fourth Quarter	Total Year One	Total Year Two
Gross revenue sales						
Other revenue						
Direct expenses						
Indirect expenses						
Net profit						

Lessons Learned

Take a minute to consider what you have learned from this long process—from idea to enterprise. Have you embedded some or all of these new business practices into your day-to-day organizational management structure? Capture these thoughts and ideas before they are lost so you can commit to systemic change and improvement.

Worksheet Thirty-One: Lessons Learned and Resources Needed

> ### Don't Go Back to Business as Usual!
>
> You have invested an incredible amount of time and effort into this social enterprise process, learning valuable new skills and developing a new and more efficient way of conducting your organization's business.
>
> **warning!**

What are the most important things you've learned?

◆ _____

◆ _____

◆ _____

◆ _____

◆ _____

What will you do differently as a result of the social enterprise process?

◆ _____

◆ _____

◆ _____

◆ _____

◆ _____

What resources do you need to succeed?

Technical Resources	Knowledge Resources	Other Resources	Plan to Develop Needed Resources

To Recap

◆ A business plan is a vital part of the social enterprise process.

◆ Don't go back to business as usual. Instead, embed new business practices into your day-to-day management processes.

◆ Identify the ongoing resources you will need to bring your social enterprise to reality.

Chapter Ten

Sustainability: The End Goal

IN THIS CHAPTER

··→ The case for support for social enterprise

··→ Why social enterprise is a vital alternative

··→ Why is sustainability important?

··→ Case studies and stories of social enterprise ventures

Throughout this manual, we've maintained that economic business models can be applied successfully to solve our social issues. We believe it's time for charities to take the brakes off and leave traditional funding as their only model behind. It is with this in mind that we have written this hands-on manual to guide your efforts toward a more businesslike approach to managing your nonprofit tax-exempt business and to becoming sustainable.

In this chapter, we'll offer case studies and examples of some successful ventures. Keep in mind that while not every enterprise reaches attainability, the processes in this manual have the capacity to change the entire dynamic of how your organization operates in the future. The outcome of adopting this social enterprise approach may not result in the actual establishment of a social enterprise; regardless, you will reap the benefits of operating more efficiently, effectively, and confidently. Our goal is to help you set the stage and build a foundation for a future that eliminates being entirely dependent on the whims of traditional funding sources over which you may have little to no control.

Our experience has shown that the process is complex. We know there are times you may feel overwhelmed, yet we encourage you to stay with it. The rewards are worth it. We firmly believe organizations that build sound infrastructures, involve their stakeholders, set clear goals, and

> Sustainability is the key to a nonprofit's empowerment. Social enterprise offers an integrated, comprehensive, and compelling model for building sustainability.
>
> **food for thought**

work with the processes we offer will get out of the charity-think rut and build a sound basis for future economic stability and sustainability.

Change Your Thinking

Establishing nonprofit management systems that are not sustainable is no longer an option.

Dan Pallotta, the author of *Uncharitable: How Restraints on Nonprofits Undermine Their Potential* and *Charity Case: How the Nonprofit Community Can Stand Up For Itself and Really Change the World*, says: "The fundamental basis for the system, by itself, is deeply flawed. Some nonprofits can barely function, all in the name of frugality and the ethics we hold so high. What if we don't need a deprivation mentality for charity? We need to stop putting the brakes on the system."

We agree with him. As we have said throughout this manual, for too long, nonprofits have operated from a system that imposed restraints and undermined their potential. The systems that kept philanthropy alive as a viable process for solving social concerns worked for many years, yet the increasing demands for services, imposed by economic downturns, government funding cuts as a result of those downturns, and more demands for social services, are causing a system breakdown.

Organizations absolutely cannot continue to operate as usual if they want to remain viable. To stay vibrant, to meet your objectives, new tools must be looked at, social enterprise being one of them. It's time to analyze if you're on track and seriously examine the challenges and stresses that may prevent you from moving forward as effectively as you'd like to. It's time you stopped ruminating over "we have a problem" and started seeking solutions. Congratulations on getting this far!

The Case for Social Enterprise

You've probably asked:

◆ How can we continue to operate this way?

◆ How will we meet the escalating needs of our community?

◆ Is this a culture we want to continue to live with?

Social enterprise can open the door to new opportunities for long-term growth and resources that lead to sustainability. We can't emphasize enough how vital sustainability is to your nonprofit's ability to work unencumbered by worrying about keeping the lights on. Another one of those prickly questions often asked and still not resolved is: Why have social issues not gone away? Instead, they continue to escalate. Certainly, nonprofits mean well and are doing their very best to achieve their mission and work toward the common good, yet the issues are still there. We believe the system itself restrains charities.

We realize that as long as there are people who have needs, those concerns will always need to be to be addressed. Dan Pallotta, a passionate advocate of business-model thinking, challenges the status quo by asking, "Does the system work? Is it the best system we could have? What other systems are available?" Dan believes we "have to free charities… from a set of rules that were designed for another age and purpose."

> *Does the system work? Is it the best system we could have? What other systems are available? [We] have to free charities… from a set of rules that were designed for another age and purpose.*
>
> Dan Pallotta

The possibility that there is another system that takes philanthropy to a different level needs to be examined and put to use. Social enterprise helps us achieve economies of scale that can revolutionize the funding system for tackling the social issues nonprofits are faced with on a daily basis. The old systems, established by our founding fathers and based on benevolent paternalism, need to be substituted with free-market "conscious" capitalism and entrepreneurship. Social enterprise is a tool for leveling the playing field and giving nonprofits like yours the possibility to determine and to govern your own future.

Why Social Enterprise Is a Vital Alternative

Most of the restraints imposed on nonprofits are economic in nature. Social enterprise allows for integrated, comprehensive systems that encourage earned revenue streams and apply market-based strategies to today's social problems. It requires structures and the resources that produce results and has a balance of mission and market, heart, head, passion, and practicality. Some, but not all, nonprofits have the resources that are above and beyond what is needed every day just to keep the doors open. You have products and services that can be leveraged to create social and economic value to attain sustainability. You'll hear from several nonprofits with their perspectives in a few pages, which may give you further ideas for your own.

Sustainability: Sustainability is the capacity to endure and continue indefinitely so that your organization produces more revenue, resources, and tangible results, with the end goal of meeting your mission and impacting meaningful social change.

Why Is Sustainability Important?

Sustainability is predicated on recurring revenue. It requires the structure that examines what works, analyzes why, and allows for the resources that produce results. It requires the toughness to discontinue the programs that don't work and won't get you to achieving your organization's goals.

Sustainability stops the vulnerability cycle. It is a challenging proposition that requires absolute crystal-clear thinking about your organization's goals and places a financial value on the achievement of those goals. It requires robust infrastructures with the capital necessary to meet overhead, sturdy information systems, financial systems, skilled employees, and fundraising processes as well as the technology to support success.

Yes, sustainability is the end of "charity-think" and the full embracing of "business-think" while recognizing that you are a nonprofit devoted to achieving your mission and creating social and economic value.

Case Studies and Stories of Social Enterprise Ventures

We've included the following case studies of a couple of organizations we've worked with to show how the social enterprise process can have far-reaching benefits to a nonprofit. They illustrate very different outcomes. Following these case studies are examples of several social enterprise ventures launched as a result of our *Expedition* process.

Case Study One

This first case study represents the far-reaching benefits of the social enterprise process we've described in this manual. Not only can this process result in a business plan for earned income, but other lasting benefits can occur as well. These include leadership development, enhanced teamwork, barriers broken, formal and informal collaboration models created, mutual support systems established, management skills strengthened, discipline, programming, new understandings of market needs and market trends, enhanced stakeholder communication, and a more efficiently and effectively managed nonprofit organization that can welcome and embrace change.

In this case study, an entirely new entity was formed to manage the business ventures benefiting several separate nonprofits.

The participants: nine independent regional 501(c) (3) heritage/tourism organizations with a single large federal/state funding source. Individual organizations have executive directors, small staff, and independent local boards of directors.

The Situation

Anticipated large reduction in or total loss of primary state/federal funding by the end of fiscal year 2013 (up to $75,000 per organization).

The Social Enterprise Journey

Session One, September 2011

Representatives from both board and leadership staff of all nine organizations first met to explore separate opportunities for earned income to sustain their organizations in response to the threat of funding reduction or loss.

While the organizations had usually communicated and cooperated superficially, they had never fully collaborated on a single venture. Issues of turf, control, and even confidentiality began to surface.

In the first full-day meeting, the facilitator led the independent teams to explore their missions and core values and then to identify each organization's knowledge and technical and physical assets.

Throughout the meeting, there were forays into discussions of whether to remain independent or to find a way to build a new business model that would combine resources under one operation. While the discussions were lively and honest and not everyone was fully invested in the end goal, the result was an informal agreement to collaborate moving forward.

Following are the session one outcomes:

◆ A guiding vision statement was developed to encompass the purpose of all organizations on the road to sustainability: "All [state] residents can connect with their roots, and all visitors can experience the [state] story."

◆ An inventory of statewide organizational assets represented by all nine agencies was developed.

◆ Teams were established to begin market research with clearly defined groups of agency stakeholders, sharing the research results among all teams.

◆ Each organization would propose potential earned income ventures at the next meeting, based upon their initial market research and asset inventory.

SESSION TWO, FEBRUARY 2012

In this second meeting, further research was shared and several potential earned income ventures were proposed as a result of the initial stakeholder research.

Objective decision-making criteria were agreed upon to assess the initial feasibility of the potential ventures, which leveraged the individual and collective organizational assets.

There was further discussion about the feasibility of remaining independent or establishing a formal collaboration to achieve the goal of sustainability. No decision was reached. As expected, some of the discussions revealed some discomfort and unwillingness as to division of labor, a sense that, historically, some players had done more than others, and the perception from some participants that a true formal collaboration could not likely be achieved.

Following are the session two outcomes:

◆ Agreement was reached to continue an informal collaboration on earned income, while each organization would also continue to explore individual income opportunities.

◆ Ground rules were established for participation in research and feasibility studies and, even further, establishing agreement that any participating organization could drop out of the process at any time without rancor or repercussion.

◆ Based on the objective decision-making criteria, thirty-one potential income ventures were reduced to three for further research and feasibility. Three cross-organizational teams were established, with team leaders identified to carry forward with feasibility studies and homework guided by the facilitator. The three social enterprise ideas were: (1) tours and tour support services; (2) a media network promoting heritage and tourism; and (3) an administrative fee for services to manage a statewide visitor pass program.

Homework and Internet Meetings Between Sessions Two and Three

As expected, some teams and team leaders progressed quickly through the research and feasibility studies, while others lost momentum and focus. Several live Internet team meetings were facilitated to assist in focusing efforts and achieving results.

Throughout this interim period, there appeared to be a new and open spirit of collaboration between the original separate nonprofits. At this point, one organization opted to pull out of the collaborative effort to explore its own earned income opportunities. Also during this time period, one of the original executive directors left her organization to pursue further education, reducing the total participating members to seven of the original nine.

The remaining teams and team leaders progressed with research to verify the feasibility of the three earned income venture ideas.

Session Three, May 2012

Board and staff representatives of the seven independent nonprofits met for their final meeting with the facilitator.

The three cross-organization research teams presented results of research findings on the three venture ideas and verified the potential feasibility of all three earned income ventures, although the research had modified some of the initial ideas to some extent. Additionally, all teams discovered valuable information that will be incorporated into their current operating structures, programs, and services to better serve their missions and take advantage of their changing marketplaces.

No separate organizational ventures were proposed at this point.

Clearly, the last hurdle to be overcome was developing a business model for the three earned income ventures. Questions remained to be answered, such as:

◆ Would one of the nonprofit organizations be paid to manage the businesses, or would management be divided?

◆ How would the business expenses be assessed? How would profit be divided?

◆ Could these new business ventures succeed under the current independent organizational structures?

It was clear to all participants that a new business model was needed and that formal collaboration was required to achieve the initial financial goals set several months prior.

Following are the session three outcomes:

Total and enthusiastic agreement resulted in a plan to establish an LLC to complete the business plans for the three earned income ventures and manage the business ventures going forward. The following was decided:

◆ Expenses and profits would be shared equally among the founding LLC partner/members.

◆ Initial investment of $5,000/agency would be confirmed by the participating organizations' boards of directors by July 1, 2012, and a first-year (2013) investment of up to $5,000 per partner/member was required to cover expenses of setting up the LLC and other initial costs to be incurred.

◆ An RFP would be developed by the LLC to contract with a business manager and to explore contracting with an independent business consultant to facilitate completion of the three or four initial business plans.

SUMMARY AND CONCLUSIONS

Initially, nine independent nonprofit organizations were forced to consider new revenue sources and funding paradigms in response to serious threats to their existence as a result of potential losses of up to $75,000 each from their traditional funding sources.

While the independent organizations historically had met often, there existed a sense of competition, some level of mistrust, reluctance to share assets and resources, some "score keeping," and no history of formal collaboration.

Additionally, while these organizations shared an overriding mission and purpose of promoting and sustaining heritage and culture, their programs were regional and they collaborated only sporadically.

There existed a type of entitlement mentality, reinforced by the funding source, that had not prepared the independent organizations for the drastic changes required if/when funding levels decreased dramatically or were discontinued all together.

Case Study Two

This case study resulted in a market-driven redesign of current programs and services. It is a good example of how embedding sound business principles into current organizational programs can result in "found revenue" without launching a new social enterprise venture.

Description of Agency

The family-centered membership agency is based in a metropolitan area of a midsized city.

The Social Enterprise Process

In January 2008, the agency participated in formal guided training about the social enterprise process.

Initially, the agency's enterprise team wanted to develop an earned income venture to support the ongoing overhead expenses for the agency. They brainstormed many potential ventures. About midway through the process, the team shifted gears and focused on how it might reduce the annual losses in membership rather than start something new.

A Change in Direction

The enterprise team undertook market research about the agency's membership and developed a series of online surveys and focus groups of current members, lapsed members, and nonmembers to determine what the agency needed to do to sustain and grow its membership numbers. The results of this thorough market research took the team completely by surprise as it tested its long-held assumptions about what benefits people wanted in their membership.

Based on its market research and feasibility studies, the agency team redesigned its membership benefits, focused on the atmosphere at the agency, and refocused on personal attention and individualized plans, all of which were directions supported by current, former, and potential customers. The agency committed to budgeting revenue to support media and marketing efforts to encourage membership based upon the results of its market research and increased growth and retention.

As a result of this new direction, the agency exceeded its first-quarter membership goals by over $4,000 and more than doubled its revenue goals for the second quarter. Growth continues with a steady influx of new members, and the agency's member-retention factor has dramatically increased. Now that the importance of market research has become embedded in the agency's management culture, it continues to survey existing clientele, shop its competitors, and reevaluate programs each quarter. This is an ongoing process that should continue to support growth.

A Sampling of Outcomes

This list describes the social enterprise results for several different nonprofit organizations with whom we have consulted. Thousands of other examples can be found on the Social Enterprise Alliance website at se-alliance.org.

Following are examples of some of the agencies/missions and their outcomes:

◆ Agency that provides direct services to adults with disabilities opens a certified organic greenhouse business, providing products to local retail and industrial businesses and employs clients.

◆ Botanic gardens rent the gardens for special events with a menu of additional services using its commercial kitchen and other facilities.

> *The social enterprise process helped our agency focus more on building a solid business plan for our existing enterprise (membership) based on the wants and needs of our clientele. The stakeholder, member, and community surveys were true eye-openers as to what our clientele really wanted. We used those suggestions to build an enhanced membership program that we implemented and began promoting in December 2008. Our membership numbers have begun steadily growing and the response from the new participants has been very positive.*
>
> D. Wright

◆ Agency that provides before and after school programs revises traditional programs to meet market-driven needs of special and underserved populations discovered in their market research.

◆ Residential program for families of cancer patients brings a vehicle donation program run by an out-of-state for-profit in-house, leveraging relationship assets for business planning. It manages a used-car lot and monthly auction as well as consignments from other nonprofits.

◆ Transitional housing for ex-offenders opens a thrift and furniture resale store.

◆ Agency that provides in-home meals for seniors opens a cafeteria and catering business.

◆ Day shelter program for homeless individuals opens a coffee shop in a busy downtown commercial area with a training program for clients.

◆ Outreach program for youth and young adults starts fee-for-service consulting programs.

◆ Health and wellness agency offers fee-for-service programs to other nonprofits.

◆ Training program for disabled adults earns a management fee from a state contract to package and distribute transportation passes.

◆ Family and child counseling agency develops employee assistance programs for corporate partners.

◆ Faith-based family counseling program offers faith-based continuing education for medical professionals.

◆ Transitional program for ex-felons opens a landscape business, training clients and providing services to businesses and individuals.

◆ Agency purchases run-down properties, rehabs them, and rents them for income.

◆ Agency leverages its expertise in weatherization services for low-income clients into providing services for commercial property owners.

◆ Agency modifies its financial literacy program for low-income clients into programs for businesses and their employees.

◆ An agency serving adults with disabilities expands its single greenhouse into several greenhouses, qualifies as a certified organic greenhouse, trains clients, and provides produce for local businesses and industry cafeterias.

◆ A respite program for handicapped adults opens a day care in an underserved community, providing programs for handicapped and nonhandicapped children.

◆ Historic cemetery establishes a memorial program that provides recognition at holidays and events.

Why Should Your Agency Consider Social Enterprise?

Here is what agency leaders have said after completing the process described in this manual.

◆ "During these challenging economic times, [our agency] has had to face the hard truth that our faithful regular funders are unable to fund at past levels, sometimes not at any level. If it were not for our vehicle-donation program, we could not continue the excellent programs and services for our guest families. The time and money our social enterprise team invested in training four years ago has certainly proved to be well worth it!"

◆ "It was a great time of reflection and assessment for us to really look internally at our assets, at our capital, to affirm our core. All of that was very helpful. It gave us perspective."

◆ "It is okay to collect money from people you provide services to. Social enterprise and entrepreneurial ideas give your clients more opportunities, either from the money that you bring in or from the jobs it gives to people. It has worked both ways for us."

◆ "We found that the market we thought was interested really was not or already had the need taken care of. It's teaching us the value of research and continuing to dig deeper on our ideas. Most of all, it's showing us to follow where the research leads."

◆ "We believe in the process. It was like a sermon! It gave us a new way of thinking. How can we sustain our programs? In social service, there is the old way of doing things: We depend on the grant; we depend on the state and federal funds. Now it is: Okay, you can self-sustain; you can depend on you."

◆ "*Free* has changed to *fee*. We have changed everything in our thinking."

It's been obvious for some time that the current model of philanthropy is broken. For many nonprofits, funding from traditional sources, such as the federal government, corporate funders, and foundation funders, has shrunk or even disappeared.

Those organizations that for years and years have relied on "renewing the grant" and an annual campaign or event to fund vital programs and services are now faced with the dilemma of finding new revenue sources, which may no longer be available, or reducing staff and cutting back on programs and services.

Nonprofits can no longer continue to rely on past efforts. Today's more challenging environment calls for fundraising strategies based on quantifiable research and proven methodology.

> Now the warnings are louder. Nonprofits are hearing "no" more often. They are having to wake up to the fact that it is way past time to take responsibility for themselves, to seek and secure new sources of revenue, especially those sources that the agency can control to a greater extent.
>
> **warning!**

The competition and a dramatically different funding landscape require a laser-like attention to methodologies that work. Crossing fingers and wishful thinking were never highly probable; today it's impossible.

Dependence or Independence?

We can promise you that the *entitlement* generation of nonprofits is now faced with a steep learning curve that will rock it to its foundation. The new generation of nonprofit leadership *must* be realistic and must take responsibility for its own capacity and sustainability. They *must* be willing to look at a higher form of collaboration than ever before. They *must* be willing to put traditional turf issues aside and work for a greater purpose.

Complacency can no longer remain the norm. "Things aren't perfect, but at least this way of operating is what we know. We have learned to work within the entitlement process and have managed to make it work for us. Besides, what else is there?"

This mindset doesn't work any longer. Not that it ever really did.

The history of traditional funding has encouraged nonprofits to rely on others to sustain them, to become less and less self-reliant, to take less and less responsibility for their futures. We believe it's time to implode that type of charity-think. It's time to think big. It's no longer about raising a little bit of money, just enough to get by, keep the doors open, and fulfill the mission, but about having consistent dollars that allow for renewed self-confidence and the self-governance necessary to fulfill new dreams.

To Recap

◆ Social enterprise applies market-based approaches to address the many social and economic issues and seeks solutions to these concerns that are sustainable—rather than relying on philanthropic or government funding.

◆ Social enterprises come in many shapes and entities: revenue-generating businesses, nonprofits, for-profit organizations, government entities, or hybrid organizations.

◆ Savvy nonprofits have learned to operate in a more businesslike manner that protects their valuable programs and services from the whims of donors, economic slowdowns, and federal budget issues. They have begun social enterprises. They have taken charge of their funding.

Appendix A

Business Plan Example: Upscale Resale Women's Clothing and Accessories (Preliminary Draft)

(Reprinted with permission of Casa Esperanza.)

Social Enterprise Mission Statement

To offer to the community the opportunity to purchase high-end, gently used clothing and accessories in support of the patient navigation program at Casa Esperanza.

Agency Mission Statement

Casa Esperanza is the house of hope and home away from home, providing a caring community to support and serve families facing cancer.

Executive Summary

History of [the agency]

[The agency] opened its doors to [the state's] cancer community seventeen years ago and has a strong legacy of providing a home for families struggling with the realities of cancer treatment. Our mission is simple: to provide a caring environment and support services for cancer patients and their families who must travel for treatment. Since 1992, we have provided housing and support for more than 25,000 families.

In 2006, [the agency] was fortunate to receive a grant from a trust to fund a pilot program for patient navigation. National studies indicate that there is a significant need for patient education on available social services and that if more patients fully understood the services available, their quality of life and longevity may be significantly improved. Hugely successful in terms of use by our clients, the patient navigation program is in search of greater financial sustainability. Currently, the program is dependent on grants and private donations, and the current economy makes obtaining such funds more competitive and harder to secure. Funds raised above and beyond the expenses of the program will be used to fund other client support services at [the agency].

Table of Contents

Hope Couture Description

The focus of Hope Couture is to create and build upon a base of consistent donors of gently used high-end women's clothing and accessories. To provide the [specific target] communities with a positive experience and awareness of [the agency] as they purchase high-end merchandise. To utilize revenue from sales of donated gently used high-end women's clothing and accessories to support the patient navigation program and other client support programs at [the agency].

Business Philosophy

We believe that there is a ready market for high-end, gently used women's clothing and accessories, especially given the current state of the economy.

Focus Areas

- ◆ Customer base
- ◆ Factors of success
- ◆ Our products
- ◆ Market research
- ◆ Economics/financials
- ◆ Promotion
- ◆ Location/costs
- ◆ Organizational details

Short-Term Objectives and Long-Term Goals

In order to achieve the long-term goal of growing a viable retail business, in the short term, there will be benchmarks to reach, such as:

- ◆ Daily, weekly, monthly sales goals
- ◆ Marketing plan for two-month intervals, such as postcards, opening press release, email announcements of special in-shop events
- ◆ Procedures set up and tested before grand opening
- ◆ Grand opening [date]

Who Is the Customer?

The customer is generally a woman twenty years old or older. We are focusing on the upscale retail customer who is looking for both professional and personal clothing.

Benefit to the Customer

Obtain excellent products at a fair and below-market price. Merchandise prescreened and cleaned for value/quality. Emphasis on good customer service and satisfaction. Knowledge that highly ethical business and marketing practices are in place. Awareness that purchases will benefit others—"Buy for Good" philosophy.

Products

Hope Couture—Upscale Resale Boutique

A market for donated gently used high-end women's clothing as well as donated accessories. All items placed in the store will be screened for value, condition, and consumer interest. All care will be given to avoid less than desirable apparel and to create a reputation for excellent quality at an affordable cost, with emphasis on exceptional customer service.

Consignment Sales Service

We will provide floor space for individuals to place their items in our store at a 40 percent share of the sale to [the agency].

Merchandise Delivery Service

We will offer free pickup service for donated items from donors within the greater metropolitan area.

Displays/Sales of Artwork

We will invite our artists, those who have been involved with [the agency's annual art fundraiser], to display their artwork on a rotating basis. We will not charge a commission from sales of these pieces but will offer the opportunity to host a monthly or quarterly "opening" event to feature each artist, inviting special friends, donors, and area merchants to attend. This will promote both the artists and Hope Couture's current inventory. We will also be able to keep the displayed items fresh and new for shoppers.

"Buy for Good" Thrift Guide

We will work with [collaborative agency] antique store and other nonprofit thrift businesses to produce a guide to highlight all of the cause-based resale stores.

Target Donors

[The agency] has a large donor list that will be a crucial part of the business as well as community outreach with organizations to help to clothing drives. We have relationships with many artists we will do consignment with to help complement the clothing business.

Competitive and Complementary Businesses

The most similar businesses are [several local competitors named]. However, we will specialize in upscale women's clothing and accessories, which will set us apart from others.

Factors That Will Support Success

Taken from articles found on Google:

Thrift Stores and Consignment Shops

"Mar 3, 2009 . . . The profile of resale shops like Celery continue to rise with the economic downturn."

"Resale and thrift shops are helping to reduce waste, energy use, and greenhouse gas emissions across America. They are also creating jobs, and increasing economic prosperity in many communities. According to the National Association of Resale and Thrift Shops, these shops are generating over $200 billion in revenue every year."
pnj.com/apps/pbcs.dll/article?aid=/20080602/life/806020304/-1/archives

"Approximately 16 percent of all shoppers buy secondhand items at thrift stores and this percentage is expected to rise to 20 percent very soon. The demand for secondhand items has been the catalyst for a 5 percent annual growth in resale and thrift shops in the past few years."
pnj.com/apps/pbcs.dll/article?aid=/20080602/life/806020304/-1/archives

"Even local governments are opening thrift shops. The Palm Beach County Thrift Store (PBCTS) sells surplus government property, mink coats, sheriff's department evidence, jewelry, unclaimed items, golf clubs that were donated to the school, and many other items. The PBCTS is a municipal investment recovery cooperative involving twelve area local governments. The PBCTS has served the area for fifteen years and has generated over $20m for the taxpayers of Palm Beach County."
pbcgov.com/fin_mgt/store
bizjournals.com/southflorida/stories/2000/10/30/story6.html

The retail establishments that sell secondhand items go by many names. They are called thrift stores, charity shops, reuse shops, consignment shops, used furniture stores, secondhand stores, etc. The concept of formally selling secondhand goods in retail stores started in the late 1940s when OXFAM opened a store in the United Kingdom. Many thrift stores are associated with religious organizations, yet many are secular as well. The charity status of many thrift stores in the United States provides a significant benefit for taxpayers by providing a tax deduction for the items donated to the charity shop.

The local economic benefit of thrift stores can be seen in many ways. Local jobs are created when these stores open, affordable products are made available to people who can't afford to buy new products from retail stores, landfill costs are reduced, the release of greenhouse gases and other pollutants are reduced, and local sales tax revenues increase.

Other forms of resale and nonprofit organizations also have positive economic and environmental impacts in the community. The Alachua County Library Book Sale sells used books from its archives and books donated by library patrons to generate money to invest in new books for the library district. The Dignity Project takes old cars and computer equipment and refurbishes these items for donation to economically disadvantaged people in Gainesville. These products help people prepare for jobs and provide transportation for these folks to work and other destinations.

Specific Factors to Hope Couture That Will Support Success

Availability of items/clothing/merchandise to be donated and sold:

◆ Donors

◆ Art/vendors

◆ Estate closeouts

◆ Consignments

◆ Partnerships with groups such as CREW (Commercial Real Estate Women)

◆ New attitude about resale/consignment due to economic condition

◆ No cost for donated items/merchandise being sold (all sales at a profit)

◆ Additional opportunity for revenue for consigned articles

◆ Partnerships in community are a priority (set standard for good service for a good cause)

◆ Fabulous location will draw from the university and retail and restaurant traffic in the area

◆ Volunteer contribution of time, talent, merchandise, and marketing

◆ Dual use/retail and intake area (lots of space)

◆ Strong, growing mission visibility (all ages)

Our Competitive Edge

Large existing donor market both for securing merchandise and for sales. Difficult economic times increase market for bargain hunters, especially women who need that "new" business suit, cocktail dress, or formal. Low overhead and labor costs, using one paid employee and a vast volunteer pool to provide labor force. Well known throughout the community as a long-standing, ethical, and financially stable nonprofit agency. Can set competitive pricing strategies and aggressive sales incentives. "Customer first" approach will provide outstanding customer service.

Advertising and Promotion

◆ Direct-mail postcards to announce store opening and new seasonal items

◆ Frequent-buyer cards

◆ Print ads

◆ Special in-shop events such as trunk shows for children and parents

◆ Gift basket donations to charity fundraisers

◆ Have the [fundraiser] artists' art in the store for three months, but once a month, feature one of the artists and invite that artist's customers

◆ Have pictures around of people at [agency] hung all around the store. Very powerful!

◆ Have monthly sale items.

◆ If we receive men's clothing, have a shopping night for the men that would also include women's clothing.

◆ Have a flyer sent to all companies [agency] has worked with about the new store so that companies can also do clothing drives.

◆ Have emails to all of [agency's] contact with employee's and board contacts about upcoming events at the store.

◆ [Area] stroll

◆ Work with restaurants in town. Maybe get discounts or do a fashion show during lunch or dinner.

◆ Postcard announcements to board contacts (databases)?

◆ Teaser openings before we formally open

◆ Feature artists and, again, advertise it.

◆ Fashion show at store with wine and cheese for public plus specified groups, i.e., realtors

◆ Press. Get TV and radio to announce.

◆ Trunk shows

◆ Take all donations, keep what we need and give away to other charities what we don't need.

◆ Art from [agency art auction] at store and fashion show

◆ Agency art auction event

◆ Cross advertise. Have one brochure or postcard with all that [agency] does—Give Hope a Ride, Hope Chest, Hope Couture, etc.

◆ Advertise on web.

◆ Raffle off an "outfit of the quarter."

◆ Build in a conference room for us to use as well as other business and charities. This will need to have an entrance or some way of closing off the store part.

Business Hours

10:00 a.m. to 6:00 p.m. Tuesday through Saturday

Location

Location is going to be very important and will need to have surrounding business that helps draw the customer. The size of the space is flexible—in the range of 1,500 to 6,000 square feet. An open floor plan would be helpful for a clothing store. A rental range of between $1,000 and $2,000 per month.

Demographics

2008 Population	One Mile	Three Miles	Five Miles
	16,326	104,502	237,101
2008 average household income	$60,085	$45,996	$48,861
Median age	35.03	35.59	36.54
Gender—male	8,048 (49.3%)	52,303 (50%)	116,712 (49.2%)
Gender—female	8,278 (50.7%)	52,199 (50%)	120,389 (50.8%)

Operational Plan

Management and Organization

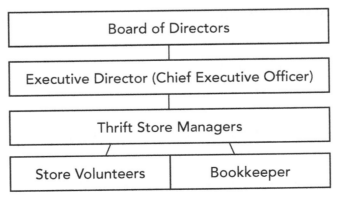

Employment Model

Employees

- Two part-time managers, five hours/day, twenty-five hours/week (full time after one year or sooner if business so warrants) at $13/hour

- Two to four volunteers per day, four-hour shifts (one or two volunteers per shift)

- Contracted bookkeeper—$200/month (raise to $400/month after first year or sooner if business so warrants)

- Existing [agency] administrative oversight

Types of Labor

- Sales clerks—volunteers

- Merchandise handlers—volunteers

- Display specialists—volunteers

- Bookkeeping—weekly reconciliations

- Marketing and PR by current agency staff

Pay Structure

- Manager—$13/hour at twenty-five hours per week

- Mileage reimbursement at current agency rate (48.5 cents/mile)

- Bookkeeper—$16.60/hour for three hours/week.

Financials

Budget—Income Data

	Fiscal Year Ten Proposed Budget	Notes
Ordinary Income/Expense		
Income		
4100 Sales Income		
4101 Direct Sales—Donated Items	85,000	
4102 Consignment Sales—60/40 Split	30,000	Art, jewelry, apparel, and accessories
4103 Sales—Other	2,500	[agency] merchandise, etc.
Total 4100—Sales Income	117,500	
4200 In-Kind Donations		

	Fiscal Year Ten Proposed Budget	Notes
4201 Donated Apparel And Accessories	90,000	
420 Donated—Other	10,000	Equipment, etc.
Total 4200 In-Kind Donations	100,000	
Total Income	217,500	
Expense		
6000 Payroll Expenses		
6001 Gross Salaries And Wages	33,800	Two part-time managers—25 hours/ week at $13/hour
6001A Bonuses	250	
6004 Direct Deposit Fees	24	
6050 Benefits Expense		
6057 Employee Assistance Program	144	
6058 Benefit Allowance Expense	0	
Total 6058 Benefit Allowance Expense	0	
Total 6050 Benefits Expense	50	
Total 6000 Payroll Expenses	34,218	
6100 Payroll Taxes		
6101 Medicare Company	494	
6103 Social Security Company	2,111	
6105 State Unemployment	100	
Total 6100 Payroll Taxes	2,705	
6200 Depreciation And Retirement		
6201 Depreciation	0	
Total 6200 Depreciation And Retirement	0	
6500 Contracted Services		
6501 Bookkeeper	2,400	$200/month for weekly audit
6502 Computer Support	400	
6505 Housekeeping	2,400	$200/month for monthly cleaning— other cleaning by volunteers
6508 Professional Fees	500	Other fees as necessary
Total 6500 Contracted Services	5,700	
6600 Mileage/Travel		
6600a Mileage	500	Encourage use of agency van/truck
6600b Gasoline	3,000	to pick up donations

	Fiscal Year Ten Proposed Budget	Notes
Total 6600 Mileage/Travel	3,500	
6700 Office And General		
6701 Office Supplies and Subs	500	
6702 Office Equip Repair/ Maintenance		
6702a Equipment Purchases	1,500	
6702c Office Computer Software	350	
6702d Office Equip Repair/ Maintenance—Other	100	
Total 6702 Office Equipment— Repair/Maintenance	1,950	
6703 Printing	1,000	
6704 Postage and Mailing	1,000	
6705 Dues, Fees, Licenses	200	
Total 6700 Office And General	4,650	
6750 Planning and Development Expenses		
6751 Planning/Meeting Expense— Internal	250	
6752 Meeting Expense Development—External)	500	
Total 6750 Planning and Development Expense	750	
68503 Volunteer Expense	0	
6800 Insurance	745	Business, merchandise, workers' comp
6900 Telephone	850	
7000 Utilities	5,000	
7001 Rent	15,000	Hoping for no more than $18,000 maximum—in negotiations
7100 Other Expenses		
7102 Staff/Volunteer Support	250	
7102 Training and Development	750	
Total 7102 Staff/Volunteer Support	1,000	
7105 PR/Promotions		
7105 PR/Promotion Expense Reimbursement (Reimbursement of PR Expense)	0	

	Fiscal Year Ten Proposed Budget	Notes
7105 PR/Promotions—Other	1,000	
Total 7105 PR/Promotions	1,000	
Total 7100 Other Expenses	2,000	
7400 Fundraising Expenses		
7410 Other Event Expense	1,000	
Total 7400 Fundraising Expenses	1,000	
8100 In-Kind Expenses	100,000	Same as in-kind income above/guess
Total Expense	177,218	
Net Ordinary Income	40,282	
Net Income	40,282	
There may be capital outlay costs for setup. Currently being investigated.		

Costs—Setup, Fixed, and Variable

Setup costs are currently being researched and will include costs for electrical wiring and lighting fixtures, nonstructural wall demolition, interior space reconfiguring, painting, conference room flooring, signage, clothing display racks, and shelves, etc. The committee is keen to see that many of these services and goods will be donated, thus reducing costs as much as possible.

Appendix B

Resources

Ashoka: Innovators for the Public—ashoka.org
Strives to shape a global entrepreneurial competitive citizen sector, one that allows social entrepreneurs to thrive and enables world citizens to think and act as change makers.

Business Plan Competition Winners, Tampa Florida—childrensboard.org/budgeting/revenues-and-expenditures/funding-opportunities

Entrepreneurs Foundation—entrepreneursfoundation.org
Various chapters throughout the world that leverage their corporate assets to create customized philanthropy and community programs that meet corporate objectives and serve social needs.

Field Study of Social Enterprise—toolbelt.se-alliance.org/resources/1914
This compilation includes the trends and developments of nonprofit organizations engaged in social enterprise. Key markets are training and education, thrift stores/retail, consulting services, food service, and the arts. The report presents a good overview and offers practical advice when considering social enterprise.

Skoll Foundation—skollfoundation.org
Benefits communities around the world by investing in, connecting, and celebrating social entrepreneurs.

Social Enterprise Alliance—se-alliance.org
International membership organization that supports and promotes social enterprise. Read Social Enterprise Briefing white paper.

Social Enterprise Ventures LLC—socialenterpriseventures.com
Provides a structured program of training and consultation in the social enterprise process. The consultants and trainers at Social Enterprise Ventures help make social enterprise a force for positive social change.

Social Enterprise Institute LLC—socialenterpriseinstitutellc.com
Full-service provider of nonprofit programs and consulting on social enterprise, governance, organizational development, ROI, and leadership. Dedicated to assisting nonprofit leaders and social enterprise practitioners in achieving sustainability, fulfilling their mission, and strengthening their processes using business for the common good.

Social Enterprise Examples—se-alliance.org/social-enterprise-examples
From the Social Enterprise Alliance.

Social Venture Partners International (SVP)—svpi.org
Bringing together worlds that do not typically overlap: grant making, volunteerism, capacity building, and entrepreneurism. Every SVP is a network of engaged philanthropists who believe and act on innovative strategies to address complex social issues.

TED Talks "The Way We Think about Charity Is Dead Wrong!"—ted.com/talks/dan_pallotta_the_way_we_think_about_charity_is_dead_wrong.html?source=facebook%20-%20.uucwemuzruj.facebook
In this thought-provoking presentation, nonprofit guru Dan Pallotta challenges nonprofits to assess themselves in a whole new way by taking responsibility for their own sustainability, and he shares examples of social enterprise at work.

Additional talks and programs featuring Dan Pallotta and social enterprise:

◆ frtv.org/2012/05/21/uncharitable-shattering-nonprofit-prevailing-paradigms

◆ The Charitable Deduction Issue: A Tax Increase on Charity—
youtube.com/watch?v=MXrT72qPBc4

◆ Philanthropy: The Business of Changing the World—
youtube.com/watch?v=YU-GkcuQHA4

The Chronicle of Social Enterprise
If you're wondering how long social enterprise has been part of the economic picture, the Social Enterprise Alliance offers a chronology of key events. Note that this includes social enterprise in both nonprofit organizations and for-profit businesses.

The Nonprofit Sector in Brief 2012—urban.org/uploadedpdf/412674-the-nonprofit-sector-in-brief.pdf
Each year, the Urban Institute surveys the nonprofit sector on sources of revenue, including grants, contributions, investments, and earned income. The 2012 report shows that earned income/social enterprise accounts for nearly 50 percent of revenue, whereas government sources, including Medicare, Medicaid, and grants and contracts, account for 24 percent. Clearly, privately earned income is a substantial piece of the funding pie.

Social Enterprise UK—socialenterprise.org.uk
Resources that support social enterprise in the United Kingdom.

Enterprise Nonprofits—enterprisingnonprofits.ca/about_social_enterprise/definitions
Comprehensive resource for social enterprise in Canada.

Harvard Business School—hbs.edu/socialenterprise
Comprehensive resource for nonprofits and social enterprise.

Center for Social Enterprise—centreforsocialenterprise.com/what.html
Another excellent resource based in British Columbia.

Case Studies of Social Enterprises in the UK from Social Enterprises UK—socialenterprise.org.uk/about/about-social-enterprise/case-studies

Publications

Harvard Business Review—hbr.org
A magazine featuring current articles and case studies applicable to both for-profits and nonprofits.

The Chronicle of Philanthropy—philanthropy.com
The newspaper for the nonprofit world offers news for nonprofit and other organizations on fundraising and state-of-the-industry technology and fundraising.

The Nonprofit Quarterly—nonprofitquarterly.org
A unique magazine focused on values-based management information and proven practices.

The Nonprofit Times—nptimes.org
A leading publication for nonprofit management.

Nonprofit World—snpo.org
A bimonthly magazine on leadership, with practical advice for nonprofit leaders.

Stanford Social Innovation Review—ssireview.org
Published by the Stanford Center on Philanthropy and Civil society. Usable, innovative knowledge for those actively engaged in social change.

Index

If you enjoyed this book, you'll want to pick up the other books in the CharityChannel Press **In the Trenches™** series.

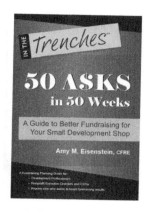

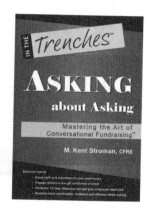

CharityChannel.com/bookstore

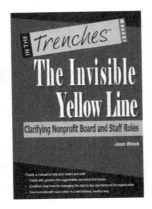

In addition, there are dozens of titles currently moving to publication.
So be sure to check the CharityChannel.com bookstore.

CharityChannel.com/bookstore

Caregiving

for the GENIUS™

Understand the Journey
from the Inside Out

Jane W. Barton

FOR THE GENIUS IN ALL OF US™

ForTheGENIUS.com/bookstore

PRESS

ForTheGENIUS.com/bookstore

PRESS

CPSIA information can be obtained at www.ICGtesting.com
Printed in the USA
LVOW03s0724090414

380981LV00011B/862/P